Through the Darkest Hour

A romantic story of a Union College man's
adventures and tribulations during
the Civil War, 1862-1865

By
LARRY HART
Schenectady city/county historian

With warm regards,
Larry Hart

Old Dorp Books
195 Droms Road
Scotia, N.Y. 12302

By the same author:
- The Sacandaga Story
- Did I Wake You Up?
- Schenectady's Golden Era, 1880-1930
- Tales of Old Schenectady, Volume I
- Tales of Old Schenectady, Volume II
- Steinmetz in Schenectady
- Hospital on the Hill
- Schenectady. . .A Pictorial History
- Best of Old Dorp
- Schenectady. . .Changing With The Times

Copyright © by Old Dorp Books
All rights reserved
ISBN 0-932035-11-6

First edition 1990
Manufactured in the United States of America

Published by Old Dorp Books, Scotia, NY
Printed by Benchemark Printing Inc., Schenectady, NY
Typeset by Silverline, Amsterdam, NY

To the memory of those who fought and died in the War between the States . . . without knowing that in generations to come, men and women of North and South would join forces in wars to uphold the inviolacy of the United States.

Contents

Prologue 8
Chapter 1: Off to War 9
Chapter 2: An Army in Waiting 19
Chapter 3: Close to the Fray 23
Chapter 4: Battle of Chancellorsville 27
Chapter 5: Home the Wounded Hero 36
Chapter 6: A Talk With Dr. Nott 43
Chapter 7: Kate's Classroom 47
Chapter 8: A Sister's Concern 51
Chapter 9: Furlough Ending 59
Chapter 10: Nashville Bound 63
Chapter 11: Battle in the Clouds 68
Chapter 12: A Visit With Seward 74
Chapter 13: Promise of Spring 79
Chapter 14: Death at Resaca 82
Chapter 15: On Atlanta's Doorstep 85
Chapter 16: A Citizen Comes Home 89
Chapter 17: Love Grows Sour 94
Chapter 18: Advice to the Lovelorn 97
Chapter 19: Wedding in New City 101
Chapter 20: The War's End 105
Chapter 21: Tragedy at Ford's Theater 109
Chapter 22: A City Bereaved 115
Chapter 23: An Ending, a Beginning 122

Contents (continued)

Epilogue 126

Appendix I: The 11th Corps and the
              Battle of Chancellorsville 131

Appendix II: Memorial Tribute from GAR 134

Appendix III: Civil War Potpourri 137

Appendix IV: The Johnsons of Union College.... 139

Appendix V: The Bounty System 140

Appendix VI: Burning of the Church 142

Illustrations

South College building on Union's campus 7
Lt. Charles Lewis and Col. Elias Peissner 17
Four poses of Katherine Rosa Smith 18
Schenectady railroad station 32
An early view of Union Street 33
The Union College campus from afar 34
Union College's famed Blue Gate 35
The "seat of stone" 42
Dr. Eliphalet Nott 46
Lewis family portraits 50
The falls at Platte Kill 55
Col. Allen H. Jackson 57
John DeBois' photographic studio 58
Joseph Hooker, the "fightin' general" 62
General Hooker's camp below Lookout Mountain . . . 67
The unfinished Capitol building in Washington 73
The Erie Canal bridge at Liberty Street 93
More family pictures 100
An 1864 engraving of President Lincoln 104
A page from Charles Lewis' diary 108
The funeral procession of President Lincoln 117
The 20th Corps in the Grand Review 121
Gravesites of the Lewises 129
The newly built First Reformed Church edifice 144

South College on Union College's campus as it looked in the 1860s. The Lewis residence was in three-story section on north end toward center. North College building is in far left background toward Nott Street.

Prologue

Back in the late 1950s, I was introduced to Charles Frederick Lewis, major of the 119th N.Y. Volunteer Infantry, when the late City Historian William B. Efner Sr. showed me the material which had just been given the City History Center through the estate of Jane Keziah Lewis Seede. As the daughter of Major Lewis, she had kept her father's military papers and other artifacts. Among them was his Civil War diary.

In addition there were family photographs stored within a typical parlor album of those times, and now I got to see the family as they looked back when Charles entered service at age 18. His father, Professor Tayler Lewis, was extremely well known by dignitaries here and in other cities.

However, after reading the diary, checking family details and other documents given the center, I got to know Charles Lewis much better. . .not as a stuffy campus brat but as a young man who had strong feelings about the brewing war between the states, Abraham Lincoln's torturous years as wartime president, the incompetence of some Union generals, and the tragedy of brother against brother in a conflict which drained North and South of the flower of manhood. He wrote often of his intense love for Katherine Rosa Smith, a school sweetheart, and his hope of becoming worthy of that love. Before the 1865 diary ended, it was evident that he considered marriage a fine institution.

The ensuring years have brought to light other matters concerning the life and times of Charles F. Lewis, to the extent that only recently it came to me that perhaps I should write his story of probably the most significant three years of his nearly 61 years of life. Few people, at a young age, could have experienced so much in such a short span — being in battles which made military history, seeing his friends die beside him in mortal combat, visiting and dining with Secretary of State William H. Seward, seeing Abraham Lincoln at encampment and in Washington City, later witnessing his death in Ford's Theater. However, I was most fascinated with his notes about Schenectady during his several furloughs home. Putting it all together, we have a glimpse of life during the Civil War, both on the battlefield and in the Schenectady area, as viewed by a student-turned-soldier.

I have often visited the gravesites of the Lewis family up in the Union College section of Vale Cemetery, and a few days before each Memorial Day have put an American flag on Charles' grave. Curious, but somehow I get the feeling that he is not really there when I set the flag staff into the ground. . .rather that there is a young man with forage cap and Union blue standing somewhere nearby, wondering why a stranger would bother. If I could, I'd tell him that I don't mean to intrude, just that their lives should not be forgotten.

— *Larry Hart*

Chapter 1
Off to War

July 1, 1862... "Today Peissner and I left Schenectady behind us, to take up arms for our cause. God willing, may we both return when the Union is victorious."

Lt. Charles F. Lewis stood proud and erect, conscious that his new uniform and officer's trappings made him look striking and a bit older than his 18 years. His deep blue campaign hat was pulled forward, shading handsome features that could not be hidden from the adoring eyes of the girl who stood beside him, her hand clasped tightly in his.

He and Katherine Rosa Smith had been betrothed only two months when word came from Washington that he and his brother-in-law received commissions in the 119th New York Volunteer Regiment, he as second lieutenant and Elias as colonel.

"Knowing that we belong to each other will make the parting easier," she had told him, but now he wasn't so sure.

That day had arrived and there were many other young men leaving from Schenectady's outdated railroad depot. The wood platform alongside the shed-like station buildings was crowded with recruits for the 91st New York Infantry, which had begun recruiting companies in upstate cities for the past month, and they were the center of family groups who had come to see them off.

Professor Tayler Lewis, cultured and eminent instructor of English and Bible interpretation at Union College, had driven the family carriage downtown that morning from their South College home. With him were his wife, Jane Keziah Payne Lewis, and younger son, Tayler Jr., his daughter Margaret with her husband, Elias Peissner, and their two small children.

Charles had walked down Union Street earlier, purposely to take one last stroll around the lower end of town before leaving its peaceful surroundings for those of guns and death. As he strode slowly, the embossed scabbard of his regimental sword swung in rhythm with his long, measured steps. It was a gift from the boys in the campus military corps with whom he trained for several months before the close of semester. On it was inscribed: "Presented to Lt. Charles F. Lewis by Members of Union Volunteer Zouaves, Schenectady, N.Y."

It was a beautiful morning, still a bit cool as grassy dew sparkled under a hazy sun. The flagstone walks of the Union Street hill were shaded by leafy elms and a delivery wagon of Pettingill & Sweet grocers was making its way over the cobblestone paving as Charles crossed to go over Lafayette Street. He was on his way to the Smith's house on Franklin Street, where Kate stayed with her widowed mother and two brothers, Edward and Maus.

And he was relieved that the boys had already gone to work so that he and Kate might have more time together before getting to the depot by 10 a.m. After a brief chat with Mrs. Smith, they made a quick departure and went up to the newly developed Crescent Park on the State Street hill above Lafayette. They sat on a wood bench, facing a downtown that was just beginning to come to life as people were walking by high-stooped homes, carriages and wagons passing in the street. But the two lovers saw none of this. They said not a word, their arms wound tightly about each other as though they'd never part.

The two had known, simultaneously, that they were meant for each other. That would have been some three years ago, when they were each 15 and attending the Union Classical department in the old college West Building corner of Union and College Streets. And it may have been that first day of class in the Higher English Department in September '59, when the two happened to be seated in separate aisles but at adjoining desks. Charles looked utterly handsome to Kate, who fairly gasped as he came into the classroom a bit late, then was assigned the desk next to hers. Despite his young age, he looked quite mature — a gangling six footer, well-developed biceps, sandy blond hair and blue eyes which seemed to glisten as he glanced her way while seating himself. He was just as stricken at first sight of her. Never would he forget the moment he looked at her as he walked toward his desk and saw her staring his way, then hastily looking aside as her cheeks flushed with embarrassment. She was small of stature, endowed with ample feminine attributes, a delightfully rounded face with tiny lips that complemented a smallish nose and light brown eyes. Long, autumn brown hair, caught by a blue satin ribbon, was allowed to envelop her slim shoulders.

The two didn't date for over a year, when finally Charles got up the nerve to invite her to a frosh party up on the campus. That was when he registered as a student at Union, class of '64. But they knew, both of them, that there would be no other.

Kate trembled and wondered if he could feel her heart pounding. As she reached up and touched his hand, squeezed it tightly, he faced her. He was silent, but his eyes gazed adoringly into hers and he leaned down to kiss her trembling lips, not bruising but insistent. When he released her, she leaned against him and buried her head against his shoulder. As his lips brushed against her auburn hair, he held her even tighter and whispered, "Kate, I shall miss you the minute I leave this place and I want you to know I'll be counting the days when I get leave to be with you again."

She couldn't answer. Her throat was tight and her mind whirling; she looked up with brimming eyes and he kissed her again. There was no thought in either mind that passersbys might be staring at lovers spooning in public, and in mid-morning, least of all the son of one of the city's socially elite families. They sat in silence, counting each fleeting moment now as though time were their enemy.

Suddenly, as a brassbound locomotive with its rumbling coaches chuffed across the grade-level rail crossing far in the distance, Charles was awakened to reality. He pulled his arm abruptly from Kate's shoulders and stood to help her from the bench. "It's time, Kate darling. The others will be waiting for us," he tried to say lightly, "and I shouldn't be a deserter on my first day of duty!"

* * * * * *

Professor Lewis tugged with nervous gestures at his white chin whiskers, much the way he would show impatience with his students in the classroom. Recently turned 60, he was slender, wiry, and his silvery hair almost touched his shoulders as it flowed from beneath a black silk stovepipe hat. The old gentleman pulled a large gold watch from the inner confines of his button vest several times as the time drew near; then, looking in the direction of the Liberty Street crossing just beyond the depot, he turned sad gray eyes to his uniformed son as if pleading for more time. A whistle blast from the west signaled that the troop train had crossed the river bridge and would arrive shortly.

He was a deeply religious man, Tayler Lewis, and now he found himself fighting emotions to keep a promise he had made to Charles at breakfast that morning. "Please Father, don't make a scene at the station," his son asked. "So many have left before this."

The coaches of the train were decked out in red-white-and-blue banners and small flags, and as the brass-trimmed engine chugged toward the depot platforms, some of the recruits on board grasped the colors and waved them with lusty cheers. Many of them hopped off, shook hands with the men on the platform and kissed the girls.

Charles embraced his mother, who was quietly weeping. Tayler Jr., who had just turned 16, but seemed younger, pumped his older brother's hand and grinned with envy. His sister Margaret, who bravely watched her husband as he held close their three-year-old daughter and infant son, turned a tear-stained face against Charles' shoulder.

"I'm afraid, dear God, I'm afraid. Please, Charles, don't take any foolish chances down there, will you? Stay with Elias and come home safe. I don't know what I'd do if. . ." Her voice trailed off into choking sobs as she threw her arms around her brother.

Kate stood briefly with the other women as the young lieutenant bade farewell to his father.

Almost a head shorter, Professor Lewis looked up into his son's face as he clasped his shoulders and solemnly recited from the Old Testament: "So let all Thine enemies perish, O Lord; but let them that love Him be as the sun when he goeth forth in his might."

It struck Charles that his father, from whom he had expected much preaching and strict admonishments, had held best to his bargain at the parting. The professor, who managed one of his infrequent smiles as he stepped back to allow Kate a last moment with her beloved, suddenly thrust an object into Charles' hand. It was his gold watch.

"Keep it with you, my boy," Professor Lewis called out, the shrill tooting of the train whistle nearly drowning his words. "Remember, we shall be thinking of you always."

Kate drew close to him. She closed her eyes as his lips came to hers and he held her in a tight embrace that took her breath away. "Kate, darling Kate," Charles whispered softly, "I'll come back to you, never fear."

The recruits had scrambled aboard, and most of those leaving from Schenectady had jumped into the nearest coaches, when Elias Peissner called to Charles.

"We had best hop to it, Lieutenant, or our regiment will win the war without us!" He had calmed his wife now to the point where she was smiling, daubing her eyes with a fancy lace handkerchief.

As the train began to pull away slowly, many of those on the platform ran alongside as far as they could, clutching an extended hand or reaping one last kiss. Charles leaned far out of the open window on his side and waved back.

There was a lonely silence after the long train had labored around Engine Hill and disappeared in the trailing smoke. Those left behind stood a few last lingering moments. Gradually the crowd of women, children and elderly men dwindled as they left with sad faces homeward, where that warm light glowed too, only to fade slowly in the coming days as the long months of waiting became a heroic duty.

* * * * * *

Kate said goodbye to the others, promised to keep in touch, then walked across the canal bridge to do some shopping as a means to help get her mind functioning once more. She walked past Van Horne Hall, next to John Burns' Sharratt House, and winced as she noted the large recruitment posters which Postmaster J.W. Veeder had hung on the theater billboards outside, appealing to "all able-bodied citizens of the North to join in our cause to protect the Union." The hall itself was being used for recruitment, training and acceptance of bounties to be paid enlistees. One of the posters announced that a total of $233,500 in bounties had been contributed thus far, which should forestall another draft for Schenectady.*

*See "The Bounty System" page 140.

The draft law had been violently attacked throughout the northern states, with some justification. Bounty brokers were cashing in on deals to arrange for willing substitutes, some who were professional "bounty jumpers", risking imprisonment by enlisting, deserting and re-enlisting to get more bounty. If conscripted, a person could buy his way out for a standard $300. If he wished to muster in, he would receive a bounty.

Groups of merchants, who had been unfolding street awnings and carrying out wares for sidewalk display, now stood about discussing the war situation. It had not been going too well for the North, and they would change it if they could.

Kate stopped in at H.S. Barney & Company's big department store a bit farther down the street, sniffed some perfume, looked at lace-fronted blouses and stylish ladies' shoes, severely pointed with genuine calfskin uppers. But nothing could get her mind off Charles, so she left and went into Mrs. Harriet Metcalf's tiny fancy goods store just below Ferry Street. Here she made a purchase. Bracelets were in fashion again and Kate was particularly struck with one made of gray bone with gold clasps.

As she made her way back to her mother's Franklin Street house, Kate tried to think of other things. This was her second year of teaching school. She was so happy to get an appointment a week after her certification, following an examination at the Union School, and she wished it could have been in the city itself. But the people out in Niskayuna were good to her, as was the school board itself, and she liked the way the pupils at Niskayuna P.S. 35 schoolhouse took to her. However, she was glad the summer vacation had just begun. There were 31 pupils and five grade levels . . . which would be too much for this particular day.

She thought, too, of when she and Charles might wed. He had just finished his second year at Union and it was highly unlikely that his father, in particular, would give his blessing to their wedding until Charles had earned his diploma and "settled down". This was the impression she got when they became engaged May 14, only six weeks ago. At a family party in the Lewis household, they agreed that the war made marriage impossible and time would dictate when it might take place. Still, Professor Lewis, wagging his finger at his son during the discussion, warned Charles: "You have much to learn, much to accomplish before you can take on marital responsibilities. You must finish college at all costs, get a position perhaps in a law office, then you might consider becoming a husband!"

Kate deeply resented the father's attitude, but she said nothing. Charles had protested mildly but let it pass, no doubt because he would be leaving shortly. "But darn it," she muttered to herself, "we're both old enough to know what we are doing and what we can do. A lot of people get married before they are eighteen!" They were both born in 1844, she in January and he in June.

As she rounded the Jay Street corner into Franklin, Kate could see her mother, garbed in her customary printed gingham dress and housekeeping apron, standing at the front doorway of their home. She was plainly upset as she conversed with a stocky, mustached man who stood at the foot of the high porch stoop.

What was brother Edward doing away from the broom factory at this hour of the morning, Kate wondered. Since the first factory burned the year before, taking with it part of the lower section of town — and their father Otis' life a few months later — Edward had assumed responsibility as head of the house and foreman of the new Cucumber Alley factory.*

Both looked up in dismay as Kate hurried to the house. Edward broke the news. "It's Maus," he said. "He's gone and joined up!'

Her younger brother had indeed joined the cause. In less than two months, they would receive word that "Pvt. Maus Smith, Co. B, 134th NY, has been killed in action against the enemy during a skirmish at Chantilly, Va., Aug. 28, 1862."

In another four months, Edward would also answer the call to arms, enlisting with the cavalry but serving less than a year before he was granted a medical discharge.

* * * * * *

As they rode along the scenic New York Central route past the West Point military academy, Charles and Elias sat comfortably in a private room of an officer's car. They had made only one stop, in Albany, and the recruits taken on there filled the cars, 15 of them, headed for New York City and, eventually, the nation's capital.

Both men sat beside a window facing out toward the Hudson River. It was nearly noon and they were having lunch — a cold plate of sardines, cheese, sliced ham and boiled eggs with a bottle of beer. They had finished talking about the rigors of leaving home and saying goodbye. Now they were discussing their future in army life, as uncertain as it might be. Elias was sure they would be all right. "Damned if we're not in the right, so doubly damned if both of us don't make it back alive!" he shouted as he thumped the side of his boot.

Elias Peissner was more than a brother-in-law to Charles, and had been ever since the older man set foot on the Union College campus four years before. He was a best friend, confidante and kind of an idol.

An impressive looking man was he, with a shock of black hair with mustache and neatly trimmed beard, tall with a slim, athletic body. His ennunciation was rapid and distinct. However, it was his wit, charming personality, and a dignified German accent which Margaret always claimed won her heart the moment she met him at a faculty party. He had come to America with another "freedom fighter", Carl Schurz, because of political unrest under Otto von Bismarck's ascent to iron rule. His background as an

*See "Burning of the Church" page 142.

astute political analyst and a professorship at the University of Breslau readily earned him a faculty position at Union as an instructor of Modern Languages and Political Economy.

It was Elias who lost no time after the outbreak of war in organizing a group of young men, recruiting them as a company bent on drilling and being prepared when the call came. He had previous military experience in the Prussian army. His was a second group of so-called Zouaves at the college. The first, which took the name Seward Volunteer Zouaves, was organized by William H. Jackson, son of Prof. Isaac W. Jackson, and young Jackson headed the group as colonel when it became Company A of the 18th New York Volunteers.

Peissner's charges, garbed in colorful uniforms of red and blue flannel, trained with an assortment of old rifles that were stashed in a gun rack within a make-shift armory on the first floor of South College's middle section.

About 80 of the 100 were students at the college. Nearly all of these students afterward became officers. All who had completed their Junior year were granted their degrees. Some of the officers would return after the war to complete their course and others who did not were later given their degrees as with the class to which they belonged. Charles would be among the last.

And it was Elias who decided to forward his credentials for a commission in the volunteers the day after Fort Sumter was fired upon, "Ach," he declared when he told the family of his sudden move, "I move to this country because I believe in its purposes and freedoms. But it must remain whole, and the only way to get it back together is to win this war. So I go to fight again for freedom!"

Charles thought hard about this and two days later he asked Elias if he could also get into uniform.

"Yes, my dear brother, if that's what you really feel — deep down inside — but you have the makings of a leader, and that's what you should be," said Elias, who promptly arranged for Charles' application for a commission.

The long train ride down to Washington was made even longer by delays in several of the yards. Military troops and equipment had the right of way, but its present bulk in the face of a tremendous build-up of Union Army strength defied logistics. As he looked out the car window in the New York freight yards, Charles was amazed at the number of cannon of all sizes, boxes of ammunition and firearms, hundreds of caissons stacked closely together — all this, and more, waiting to be shipped southward to regiments already long in the fight.

It was the first time Charles had seen such an array of battle paraphernalia but he was sure he'd soon get used to it. He jabbed an elbow at Elias as he nodded toward the piles of armament.

"It's good to know we have the tools to do the job, eh Colonel?"

"Ah yes, but all the guns in the world aren't enough if we don't do it properly," said Elias, his steel gray eyes focusing on the junior officer. "Troops can win more battles by will power and cunning than they can by fire power alone. We can only hope our generals realize that as much as some of the rebel leaders have already shown."

Much later that night, when the train arrived finally in Washington and the regiment was bivouacked temporarily in a clearing near the Naval Yard, Charles bedded down on the hard ground. He was dog tired, yet the excitement of the day caused him to spend nearly an hour looking up at the starry sky. He thought of many things, what tomorrow and other tomorrows would bring as he and the 119th began preparation for full duty. But before calling it a night, he had scribbled a brief entry in his diary, ending with "Kate is now probably in bed, and perhaps dreaming of her absent lover. Poor Father and Mother also are perhaps thinking of and praying for their soldier boy."

These pictures of Lt. Charles F. Lewis and Col. Elias Peissner were taken in Schenectady in June, 1862 before their departure.

These were taken in Mathew Brady's Washington studio two months later.

Four poses of Katherine Rosa Smith: Upper left, with her mother in 1860; upper right, from a daguerreotype in 1862; lower left, in 1863, and lower right, in November, 1864.

Chapter 2
An Army in Waiting

> *September 5, 1862... "We must ask ourselves, are we here to do honor to our country by remaining sequestered from all harm while others are doing the fighting? Here we are, ready and anxious to put our training to the test and to show our mettle as fighting men, and our biggest task is seeing to the change of picket duty. Citizens of Washington within our sight and practically in our midst could do as much."*

It had been a long tedious spell of inactivity for the men of New York's 119th, assigned to the burgeoning Army of the Potomac since their arrival in Washington, ostensibly to see action. The war had been going on, but the corps who were quartered at the capital for some months found themselves mainly in training, guard duty and lolling about. There had been great concern over a possible attack on Washington by Robert E. Lee's roving Army of Northern Virginia and the ever-cautious Gen. John B. McClellan had maintained an inordinate number of troops at his disposal to protect it.

That August had been a month of victories for Lee's united forces, especially the rout of Brig. Gen. John Pope's inglorious Army of Virginia at Manassas or Second Bull Run on August 27. But there were others, in Missouri, Tennessee and Kentucky, in which the northern troops were beaten or stalled in their tracks. Pope and Fitz-John Porter came limping back to rejoin McClellan and his army. Pope was sent west to quell Indian uprisings in Minnesota.

President Lincoln, in September of 1862, was wondering what had become of his vaunted legions who outnumbered the Rebs but seemed always to fall short of out-thinking them. In desperation, he decided to restore McClellan to full command of the Union army and "Little Mac" set about once more to defend the nation's capital from invaders. It was no idle threat, however, because Lee's troops had crossed the Potomac and were in Maryland, expecting to join forces with those of Lee's sidekick, Thomas J. "Stonewall" Jackson. The North itself heard the marching feet of Confederate troops.

Charles Lewis and his men of Company C were ecstatic when the order came on September 15th for the 10th and 11th corps to move out. Jackson, who had earlier taken Harper's Ferry, the West Virginia town at the junction of the Shenandoah and Potomac rivers, now had joined forces with Lee. Now McClellan took the initiative and surged against the Confederate left in a series of attacks beginning September 17th.

Meanwhile, Gen. Ambrose Burnside's brigades had been late in intercepting the enemy but had pushed them into Sharpsburg where the Battle of Antietam, as it was called, took place. It was among the bloodiest engagements of the war, slaughtering more than 2,000 men on either side.

"What the living hell!" Peissner erupted when news of the battle reached the troops at Stone Bridge, where they had been halted for further orders. "Why are we never in sight of the enemy, never up there on the front lines! If we had joined McClellan earlier, it would have been a clear victory for us!"

Truth was, McClellan's forces outnumbered the Confederates by more than 25,000 men. However, the always dangerous Lee had been stopped in his advance and, though he held the battleground, had little choice but to pull out and recross the Potomac. Meanwhile, reinforcements began joining McClellan and now he decided to rest his magnificent army, figuring that most of them had fought well. There were some, including the 119th volunteers, who had not fought at all.

* * * * * *

It was Lee's first major foray into Union territory, this invasion of Maryland and Pennsylvania, but there would be another in months to come — Gettysburg. Both would be aimed at the same objectives: to relieve pressure in war-ravaged northern Virginia and to gain access to abundant food and forage in Maryland and Pennsylvania.

On September 24, the troops were assembled for a march south, behind the Rappahannock and the retreating Lee, when orders-of-the-day included word that President Lincoln, the day before, had signed a preliminary Emancipation Proclamation. A lusty cheer went up and the CQs paused until it stopped before resuming the list of orders. The North had now put itself on record as far as the slavery issue was concerned.

It was the second summer of battles and death, and now it was over. There were a few Pennsylvania spot raids and battles in Kentucky and Tennessee, but the fall of 1862 went by without drastic changes in military advantage. For the South, satisfied that it had committed itself well on the battlefields, particularly in holding Richmond, it was time to regroup and rest its outmanned forces. As for the North, it had suffered many losses and still groped for a command with a winning combination.

On November 7, as McClellan was still moving slowly southward, Lincoln decided to make another change in command, ordering Burnside to replace McClellan. This didn't sit too well for many of the troops. McClellan, though notoriously cautious even when the odds seemed in his favor, was much respected by rank and file. Burnside, on the other hand, was a question mark as far as generalship went and there was mumbling that the president's move might prove a disastrous mistake.

In a few weeks, the Army of the Potomac with its new leader reached the heights at Falmouth across from Fredericksburg on the road to Richmond. Lee had already dug in among the Fredericksburg hills, waiting for Burnside's next move. The latter crossed the Rappahannock and on December 13 assaulted Lee's army. It was called the Battle of Marye's Heights but really amounted to a slaughter — again, of Union soldiers. The North, with more than 100,000 men against the South's 72,000, lost 1,284 killed, 4,061 wounded and 653 missing.

Burnside and his forces went back across the Rappahannock and Lee held his ground, each side preparing for winter quarters.

And so the year ended. Charles, Elias and other junior officers held frequent conferences to discuss the war's progress, but it did little to bolster their spirit or confidence. The 119th still had not engaged the enemy even though attached to the Army of the Potomac, so they had pitifully little to criticize as veteran corpsmen.

A grizzled sergeant of the 10th, Jonathan Bugsbee by name but who answered to "Buggsy", lorded it over his compatriots because he was one of the very few who had been in battle. The previous spring, he was in Grant's army when the Federals held the field in the Battle of Shiloh, or Pittsburgh Landing, at the expense of many men on both sides. He was within earshot of Charles one night as he was riding some non-coms of the 119th about their green military status.

"You guys are a bunch of lunkheads, and yer gonna stay that way till ya see the elephant!" Buggsy sneered, spitting tobacco juice from the side of his mouth.

Seeing the elephant. That was a phrase they'd hear often until they had been through their first big fight.*

* * * * * *

Back in Schenectady, Kate and the Lewis family were alarmed at the tenor of Charles' letters, which were becoming increasingly bitter about the unit's failure to see field action in the four months spent encamped with the McClellan and Burnside commands.

"Thank the good Lord he and Elias have been spared . . . does he want it otherwise?" they thought. However, each of them was most careful not to stress that point, rather to write that no doubt the men would be called upon soon enough to uphold the Union and its principles.

Professor Lewis told his son about a recent celebration downtown in which the Clute Brothers Foundry had been honored for its part in producing the USS Monitor, the Union's formidable ironclad that had successfully engaged the Confederate dreadnaught, CSS Virginia, formerly the Merrimac. The

*See "Civil War Potpourri" page 137.

Clute brothers plant, located along the east side of the canal between Liberty and Union streets, had been commissioned to produce a workable engine to move the Monitor's big gun turret ("the cheesebox on a raft"). It did so, with skill and good results. The two big gunboats fought a five-hour standoff battle at Hampton Roads, Va. on March 9 just past. This action saved Washington and the country from a costly blockade.

The proud father wrote to say that he attended the ceremony held at the Clute foundry, which had been decorated with bunting for the occasion. Brothers Cadwallder, John and Jethro were presented official citations from the U.S. Navy. A short speech was given by Prof. Jonathan Pearson of the Union College faculty in which he praised "the successful little Monitor" for its great feat. Hereafter, he said, "our harbors will be defended by iron gunboats with enormous guns and not by costly stone forts."

"It was a great show, Charles my boy, you would have loved it," the professor enthused.

Kate had more important things to fill her usual three pages-both sides semi-weekly letter to her sweetheart, usually ending with "I can hardly wait, my precious one, for you to come home on furlough, even if for only a little while."

* * * * * *

Now the troops of both North and South were busily engaged in setting up winter quarters on opposite sides of the Rappahannock. Charles was in charge of one of the details to cut trees and, with teams of horses, haul in logs from the surrounding woods. These were hewn to size and used for construction of log houses throughout the camp. In a few weeks, the rustic dwellings, caulked with mud, were in use by the men for warm winter's lodging.

Later, Charles would remark in a letter to home, "It is a most attractive sight after dusk, when these little homes are lighted by candle and oil lamps, and the smoke is curling upwards from the chimneys. We have built a regular settlement here and one would think we were planning to stay far beyond early spring."

Chapter 3
Close to the Fray

April 19, 1863 . . . "Saw the President several times around the camp today. He looks happy and well; what a grand homely face he has, and how nobly and unselfishly has he carried himself during these terrible years. Would to God, by some miraculous change of events, this war could come to an abrupt end . . . but this is wishful thinking and perhaps unworthy of an officer who should be concerned at present only with realistic facts. We in this corps must come to grips soon with the enemy and get some decisive victories under our belt before there is any thought of the South weakening its own will to win."

The fields and woodlands of Virginia had begun to put on the bright colors of spring. It was the month of April and the Rappahannock River flowed out of the hills at the foot of the Blue Ridge Mountains between two armies which stood facing each other, waiting since winter began for the coming of warm weather.

The Army of the Potomac was encamped at Falmouth, about one mile from Fredericksburg on the opposite side of the river. There General Lee remained with the Southern army on the site of his most recent success.

There had been big news in the Federal camp at the outset of 1863. General Burnside had gotten orders to report to the president at the White House. This he did and, on January 25, was given his walking papers. Once again, Lincoln had been dissatisfied with the strategy — or lack of it — of his appointees to the command of the Army of the Potomac. He replaced the insecure Burnside with Maj. Gen. Joseph Hooker and the fact that the latter had earned the nickname "Fighting Joe" may have given the commander-in-chief some hope that he could pick a winner.

Word got out that Lincoln was miffed by the fact that Burnside had attempted to find a crossing farther up the Rappahannock and pay General Lee a surprise visit. The trouble was that Burnside tried it on January 20, when heavy rains turned trails into quagmire. So for several days, the General fumed and stewed over the fact that wagons became hopelessly stuck and the men were grumbling over the cold and lack of provisions because many of those deserted wagons contained spoiled vittles. When the tired, bedraggled troops arrived back in camp, having accomplished virtually nothing, they were hailed by those who had stayed behind as "Heroes of the Mud March".

And again, the 11th corps was among those not chosen, just to "remain in reserve". Charles, recently promoted to first lieutenant, and his fellow officers of the 119th were not the least sorry that they missed this one.

"Let's truly face facts men, we are fair weather soldiers by choice, breeding and inclination," quipped Lt. Harvey Collum.

As for their new commander, most of the officers seemed confident that he would succeed where the other failed. Peissner, in particular, knew of him and liked his style.

"Joe Hooker will take no guff from anyone. He's quite a drinker, I hear, and is extremely boastful . . . but then, he does speak the truth when he brags. I think he will show us the way to better times, much better than we've had lately."

Also, there was a stirring in the Falmouth camp that promised a renewal of fighting. The hospitals had been cleared, regiments brought up to full strength with new recruits, ammunition and arms replenished and put in order, horses were groomed and well fed, and, probably most important, morale had been greatly restored.

President Lincoln had just visited the camp, something which was becoming a ritual with him when an unusual occasion arose. In this case, it may have been to confer with the new commander just before the army went into battle.

The president reviewed the troops and, astride a dancing brown mare, later called on regimental headquarters. It seemed his mere presence inspired the men. Cheer after cheer went up along his route and he responded gaily with a wave of his black silk hat.

His concern for the men extended beyond the immediate future. After the review, he asked, "What will become of all these men after the war is over?"

He spent much of the afternoon with General Hooker. His final admonition to "Fighting Joe" was this advice: "In your next battle, put in all your men." By a strange turn of fate, that was exactly what Hooker failed to do. It would be his misfortune only to deepen the gloom which hung over the North at that time.

* * * * * *

On April 27, the army began to move. A force was sent east of Fredericksburg to attract the attention of the Confederates, while the larger part of Hooker's troops moved secretly to Chancellorsville. The Union commander was certain this time his forces would outwit the sly maneuvering of Robert E. Lee.

Chancellorsville was like a country mansion in the center of the wilderness that stretched along the Rappahannock. Within three days, the entire field and its approaches were commanded by the 5th, 11th, and 12th corps, and Hooker felt assured of victory.

"Now the enemy must flee shamefully," he told his officers the night of April 30, "or come out and meet us on our own terms to his certain destruction."

The next day was one of waiting. Many of the men, like almost all of the 119th New York, had never been in battle and the tension grew. Peissner, regimental commander, did not show his concern if he felt it.

"Tomorrow we will show them how to fight, lads . . . and if there is a man among you who doubts it, look to the God Almighty to give you purpose. This will be the victory we need to turn the tide for the North. Ours will be the honor for having won it!"

The colonel was a great believer in freedom, having come to America from his native Munich when German liberals failed to win a democratic and unified government from Bismarck. He went directly from New York City to Fort Miller in upstate Washington County where he stayed briefly with relatives. Not long after, he joined the faculty at Union College.

Charles often recalled the first time Elias had called on his father at the South College residence. His ill-fitting clothes hung with abandon on a sparse frame. A long, thin neck seemed to sprout from an outsized stiff collar, bursting into a profusion of thick black hair, drooping mustache, long sideburns and a goatee. His gray eyes varied in expression, now intense and sparkling, then soft with tenderness or twinkling with humor.

Although only 14, and still two years away from the day he would begin classes at Union College, Charles had commanded Peissner's attention.

"The boy has the capacity and certainly the greatest of determination," Elias had told Professor Lewis as the young boy eavesdropped with beaming pride. "He will make a fine scholar."

His pleasant disposition and courtly manners soon won for the German immigrant not only the endearing friendship of the Lewis family, but also the heart of sister Maggie. The two were wed in the Old Chapel in the spring of 1858 in a ceremony performed by Dr. Eliphalet Nott.

* * * * * *

April 30, 1863 ". . . Our chances are all alike so far as we can see, but the weaver knows the threads that have done their work and are to be snapped and cut tomorrow."

That evening, as the soft glow of the campfires flitted across the grassy plateau like myriad fireflies, the men of the 119th forgot the tenseness of the day and turned to cards, letters or talk of home. Peissner was in good spirits and the officers gathered around him were enjoying heartily his stories of the Prussian Guards. He never was more entertaining, Charles thought.

Elias sat on a log in front of the regimental tent, his dusty boots stretched out lazily toward the fire before them. He was smoking his trusty long-stemmed pipe, while most of the others puffed cigars.

Lt. Henry Schwerin, who commanded Company D, called Charles aside. He had a premonition that he was going to die the following day.

"It's the end for me, Charley, I feel it . . . I want you to do something for me. Inside my blouse here is a picture of Hattie Potter, a locket she gave me, and some letters. You remember Hattie, I'm sure . . . lawyer Ben Potter's daughter . . . and they live in that big brick house at 4 Union Street. Well Charley, all I'm asking is this . . . if I fall, and it's possible, take them from my pocket and send them back to her. We never told anyone, but Hattie and I were fixin' to get married when the Rebs started kickin' up the fuss, so here I am . . . a poor unmarried soldier who just knows for sure he will never get that chance again."

Henry, the son of old Max Schwerin, who retired from his butcher shop to live out his years at 136 Union Street, usually was a fun-loving sort and Charles was actually shocked to the point where he had to pause before answering.

"Hold on there, Hank, old man . . . don't go on so about what may happen to any of us! We will be in plenty of scrapes after this one, just you see, but we can't let ourselves dwell on the unknown. If there's a slug with our name on it, so be it, but as for you, Hank, the son of a thick-skinned Dutchman, I doubt if a Johnny Reb could ever put a ball through you!"

As an afterthought, Charles promised to honor his request "if you'll do the same for me . . . just in case."

Back at the colonel's quarters, the men were getting ready to turn in because camp was to break early in the morning. How could they, or any of the thousands of men in the Army of the Potomac know that at that moment, just a few miles away, Lee and Jackson were sitting on cracker boxes before a campfire, conceiving the audacious idea of flanking the Federals?

Chapter 4
Battle of Chancellorsville

May 1, 1863... "The night is a beautifully clear moonlit one; and as I sit here by the fire, with the great mass of men asleep around me, my thoughts are away in Schenectady. We fellows may think that times are hard with us, but the dear ones at home are never free. They know not to be sure that we are here waiting for the last rising of the sun that some of us will never see, or perhaps lying cold and dead, with the same moon that shines on them so kindly, lighting with a ghastly light still faces very dear to them, and which they will never more see."

The commander of the Army of the Potomac had told his orderly to wake him promptly at 5 a.m. Joe Hooker was almighty anxious to see his 73,000-man army on the move and push through any Rebel resistance to his march to Richmond. Eating a hurried breakfast at his headquarters, a farm home called Chancellors, the general was in a happy mood.

The day before, an advance probe on the road to Richmond reported back that there was only sporadic resistance, nothing to indicate that Lee's army — minus the corps of John Longstreet and Jubal Early — was going to give them trouble. Hooker congratulated himself for leaving Maj. Gen. John Sedgwick and his 40,000 men behind at Fredericksburg to keep some 10,000 Confederates otherwise occupied. Now, he thought, the brief stopover at Chancellorsville was worthwhile. The men were thoroughly rested, in a good mood, and should suffer little casualties in skirting Lee's forces.

However, General Lee had other ideas. Unbeknown to Hooker, the Army of Northern Virginia not only included Jackson's corps but was joined the day before by the divisions of Maj. Gen. R.H. Anderson and Lafayette McClaw. Only a mile and a half from Chancellorsville, Lee and Jackson planned a strategy which would use the element of surprise to counter their lack of manpower.

Splitting that manpower still further would seem foolhardy, but the two Confederate generals were banking on the overconfidence of their enemy in drawing up a plan in which Jackson's force of 26,000 would circle to the south of Hooker and come in from the west along the Rappahannock. While Lee's remaining 17,000 would keep the Federals occupied at Chancellorsville, Jackson would counterattack on the right flank. If it worked, they agreed, the Union army would be completely disoriented.

* * * * * *

At 7 a.m. the cannonading from both sides began its death song. The companies of the 119th had struck camp and remained all that morning on the fringe of the Chancellorsville plateau. They were ready to march, but Hooker's eagerness to move out had been supplanted by the old bugaboo of the Army of the Potomac — precautionary delay. There were several brief infantry skirmishes as "feeler platoons" had been sent out to ascertain location and strength of nearby enemy forces. One reported that a large force was behind the skirmish line, not even two miles away.

"Watchful waiting, indeed," a nervous Lt. Charles F. Lewis mumbled to himself as he leaned against a cottonwood at the side of Chancellorsville road. "Hell, their artillery is weak enough to walk through. We could be halfway to Richmond by now if we had started at sunup!"

The men in his company were part of the extreme right of the entire 11th corps, strung out in a single line for nearly a mile. Most of the infantry whiled away the hours by loafing, sleeping or swapping stories. They had been there since early morning, after breaking camp, but no orders had yet been given to move out. Neither had there been any breastwork thrown up nor the slightest preparation to resist an attack.*

Shortly before noon, a heavy cloud of dust was sighted in the direction of Fredericksburg, moving ever so slowly toward the right flank of the Federals' position. It caused quite a stir among the men, but it was generally agreed that the enemy was retreating from Fredericksburg and would "make our going a bit easier, all the way to Richmond."

Charles pulled his father's hefty gold watch from an inside pocket and saw that it was now past 5 in the afternoon. Elias Peissner, at his side, eyed his junior officer with an amused smile.

"Tell me the truth now, Lieutenant," Elias chided. "Is it the exact time of day which concerns you, or do you share the feeling with most of these men that time suddenly has stood still?"

Charles would always remember the last words he said to Elias, words quoted from MacBeth. "Come what may, my good Colonel. . .time and the hour runs through the roughest day."

Years later, he would call himself a stupid oaf for uttering those words. "If only I had said something less profound, more meaningful, in what was to be a farewell to my dearest friend."

* * * * * *

The guns had been stacked and the men were either cooking or eating late mess when a field officer rode by and hurriedly dismounted at corps headquarters. General orders to move up had come at last from Hooker's command and the 119th lined up, company after company, for the advance of

---

See "The 11th Corps . . ." page 131.

Gen. Oliver Howard's 11th corps. Peissner took his place at the head of their ranks and soon the long columns of blue began to move toward the action taking place less than a mile ahead.

They were scarcely in sight of the battle lines when cries of "They're runnin', they're runnin' . . . the Johnnies are runnin'!" filtered back to the advancing troops.

The men of the 11th corps could not believe their eyes, still less try to reason that the Battle of Chancellorsville would be won so easily. But there, in the distance, could be seen several thousand graycoats hastily retreating. This was Lee's army and the "retreat" was all part of the master strategy of both Lee and Jackson.

The jubilation among the 11th corps was shortlived. There had been no cavalry or infantry pickets placed on the right flank of the great Army of the Potomac to give warning of the swift and sudden approach of Jackson's men.

"My God, look! . . . Here they come!" was Lieutenant Schwerin's startled cry. He had turned his field glass to the west and saw an avalanche of Confederate columns bearing down on them just across a gully from the plateau. As they rapidly closed in, the waning sun glinted off the bayonets affixed to their rifles.

It was just after 5:30 p.m. when Jackson broke from the woods into a paralyzing charge upon the stunned 11th corps with musket volley in such force and precision that Union men were falling before they could organize firing lines. High-pitched rebel screams soon mingled with the incessant roar of cannon and rattling musketry as the Southern forces overran the Union position.

The attack was so unexpected that it was impossible for the Federals to hold their lines against a charge which swept along like a tidal wave, leaving men, horses, mules and wagons piled in an inextricable mess.

It was truly a baptism of fire for the uninitiated. The battle grew bigger, more intense, minute by minute, and the forest gloom around them was made opaque by dust and smoke. With the incessant bursts of rifle fire from right and left, the rain of bullets hit the dried soil and raised little spurts of dust as though a summer shower had just begun.

Howard's corps fought a retreating battle for more than an hour, and the 119th was in the middle of it. Charles saw Henry Schwerin go down under the first onslaught, his body riddled by incessant volleys, but it was impossible to reach him. Hattie Potter's keepsakes went to the grave with him.

Every Confederate gun on the Union left was thundering a steady ear-pounding roar, tearing the green plain to shreds. Smoke drifted over the hills, and under its cover an avalanche of brown and gray continued to roll forward. The nightmare of this day would haunt Charles for the rest of his life.

He saw his staunchest comrade and friend, Elias Peissner, crumple like a rag doll, his right arm and clenched fist held skyward as if in defiance of death itself. The colonel had fought bravely against the odds from the very beginning of the surprise attack, standing his ground and firing his Colt revolver into the oncoming mass of Confederates until they overran his position. He fell with several other men at his side, but almost instantly was out of sight as the living continued to fight close quarters in hand-to-hand combat.

Charles, fighting with the men of Company C some 30 feet from his brother-in-law, felt a momentary pang of anguish but it quickly dissipated. This was his first brush with mortal combat and he was soon to discover that, in the heat of battle, the mind is capable only of a single function — concentrating on the enemy. In days to come, however, he would find it equally surprising to discover that vivid recollections of these terrible scenes had been stored within the mind for future reference. Many times, he would see Peissner's face suddenly turn ashen as the death blow was struck, then that awful moment when his limp body sagged to the bloody turf. It was little more than a sidelong glance, but the memory was well preserved.

As his company retreated in the direction of Hooker's headquarters at the Chancellor farm, Charles saw young Joe Carter stumble and pitch forward, his belly ripped open by a Minie ball. Private Carter was Company C's flagbearer and his clenched fists still gripped the standard as he lay there. Jonas "Pop" Carter, who left his teamster's job in Schenectady earlier that year to enlist with his son, ran up to the lifeless body and wrenched the flag free.

"Poor Joe, poor Joe!" the older man cried, tears coursing down his powder-blackened face. "By Christ, I'll save your flag, Joe!" The tattered remnant of yellow cloth, bearing a white star insignia, came back with the company that night — but not in the hands of old Jonas. For the last time, he had "joined up" with his son.

There would be more fighting the next day, as Lee sought to pursue his advantage despite the loss of Stonewall Jackson, killed by Confederate skirmishers by mistake. However, the Battle of Chancellorsville would forever be considered to be that initial confrontation in the waning daylight hours of May 2.

In about three hours of violent struggle, more than 1,500 Union soldiers were killed, 100 of them members of the 119th N.Y. The rebel advance was finally halted when Hooker threw in General Berry's division of the 3rd corps. The Confederates lost over 1,600 men but were credited with another major victory. They had stopped Hooker's march to Richmond and forced the Army of the Potomac, once again, to withdraw to the Rappahannock and lick its wounds.

* * * * * *

Mercifully, there were about 70 men left of the original 100 of Company C as Lieutenant Lewis led his group to relative safety along the road to the Chancellor farm. They had been engaged in constant battle with the enemy, often eyeball-to-eyeball, for over an hour and now they were panting heavily from fatigue, pain and excitement. Probably not a man among them was untouched by rifle, sword or gun butt. Their sweat-soaked uniforms were torn and covered with blood and dirt.

Charles, sword in hand, dared not let them pause in the retreat back to Hooker's headquarters even though they had left the heavy fighting behind them. The orders were to fall back in "orderly retreat", and they were doing just that. Rebel skirmishers were firing on those moving back up the road, so it was prudent to keep an eye to the rear and fire back in return.

The last thing Charles recalled before blacking out for several hours was a group of Rebs running up the hill road toward the retreating men, hooting and hollering at them as they reloaded on the run to fire a last volley. One of these shots struck Charles, shattering his left arm just below the shoulder. The pain was so intense, he fell to his knees in agony. He tried to get up, but pain and waves of weakness knocked him down again. Then he lost consciousness.

Schenectady railroad station as viewed from State Street in the 1860s. Note cobblestone paving, gas lamp and ground level tracks.

An early view of Union Street, looking westward down the hill from Union College's Blue Gate.

The Union College campus can be seen in far background in this eastward view of the late 1860s. The foundation of the Nott Memorial building, completed in 1878, is between the North College building at upper left and South College building at upper right.

Union College's famed Blue Gate in olden times, as viewed from Union Street.

Chapter 5
Home the Wounded Hero

May 31, 1863 . . . "Left the capital this morning, on my way back home after nearly a year's absence. How much has happened since then. We have lost loved ones, whom we now mourn but bless for what they have brought into our lives. Oh, how I despair of going home, to tell them as best I can how fate has dealt them this blow."

On the passenger deck of the Hudson River Dayliner, "Isaac Newton", Charles leaned heavily against the railing with his right arm and gazed dully into the foaming waters churned by the ship's 40-foot paddle wheel. His hair, now bleached to a scraggly yellow, rippled in the slight downstream breeze. His left arm, in a black cloth sling, hugged a blue tunic partially unbuttoned against the late afternoon sun.

He was Captain Lewis now, breveted while he was stewing and fussing in the Washington infirmary. An officer of the U.S. Military Command stopped by one afternoon, some three weeks after Charles had been there, and presented him with the brevet order, a set of captain's insignia and a citation for "action in the battlefield above and beyond the call of duty".

He accepted the promotion with gratitude, but was quite frank about the citation.

"You must understand that I was out there, along with thousands of other men, all doing our level best just to save our skins. We were no heroes, just luckier than those poor bastards who didn't make it. They're the martyrs, the heroes who should be honored . . . not us!" And he handed back the citation, signed by Gen. Henry W. Halleck, general-in-chief of all Union armies.

Now he was on his way home, aboard the river steamer, for an extended medical leave. The chief medical officer wished him well and said the order he signed was for two months' furlough, but "when you check in here August 7, we might determine that you're still not ready for active duty . . . time will tell."

Alone with his thoughts, Charles let his mind wander with abandon though he had difficulty focusing on anything in particular.

"You're a mighty fortunate young man. Maybe you've lost some of the use of that arm, but you could well have lost your life," the army surgeon told him as he was ready to be removed from the field hospital tent back in Chancellorsville. Charles had been helped there by two of his men after one of them hastily applied a tourniquet near the shoulder to stem the flow of blood gushing from his arm.

In less than an hour, he had undergone surgery while anesthetized with ether. Maj. Roy Scrafford, whose walrus mustache and mutton chop whiskers looked ridiculous beneath his white surgeon's cap, stopped by later that night to see Charles in the open-sided tent to give him two pieces of news. One, that his wound would heal but, because the ball shattered about two inches of the arm bone, might cause his left arm to be partially useless. Two, he was to be sent out shortly with a caravan of army wagons, carrying some 200 wounded men, bound for the Carver Hospital in Washington.

Major Scrafford was direct. It was obvious he had been very busy and still had lots to do. In the half-light of a flickering oil lamp, beads of sweat glistened on his forehead and pouches under his eyes were underlined by the deepened shadows. His white coverall was spattered and smeared with telltale red.

"We are sending out only non-critical cases on this trip. We have plenty of wounded still not cared for, and the worst of them never could make the trek. Good luck, soldier."

* * * * * *

Early the next morning, after two hours by bumpy ride along rutted roads and three hours by troop train loaded with battle casualties, Charles was in a hospital bed with clean white sheets. He was sitting up, his back supported by two huge pillows, and as he looked around the dimly-lighted ward room was suddenly aware of its immense size. There must be about 200 beds in all, two rows with an aisle in the center, and, as far as he could see, all were in use. Some of the men were asleep or sedated, many of them groaning and stirring fitfully.

They hadn't seen much of the city on the way in because the street lamps had been snuffed out just before daylight. The way he was feeling, he didn't particulary care.

He told himself he probably was one of the luckier ones in the ward, but dammit, how his arm throbbed and ached! The bone had been partially set, the doc told him, but it would be very painful for a week or two, then it would be up to Mother Nature to knit the bone and determine what use it might be for the rest of his life. The upper part of his arm had been bound tightly with gauze wound around two pieces of lath, and the injured member was caught up in a sling tied about his neck.

At the earliest opportunity, he had checked on Elias Peissner and Henry Schwerin. Was there any possibility they survived the onslaught, were not dead after all? "No," the answer came back to his hospital bed.

Schwerin's body was not among those identified on the Chancellorsville field when hundreds of mutilated remains were removed two days after the initial battle. He was buried there with the "unknowns".

Peissner's body, found and identified after considerable delay, was sent home, arriving in Schenectady on May 20. Services were held in the college chapel, Charles learned from sister Margaret, with an address in German delivered by Rev. William F. Schwilk, pastor of the German Reformed Church, and an address and prayer by Dr. Edward E. Seelye of the Dutch Reformed Church. Elias was buried in the cemetery of the Fort Miller Dutch Reformed Church near Gansevoort. Next to his was the grave of Keziah, the first-born of Elias and Maggie, who died in 1860.

Then there was Kate . . . who was nearest in his thoughts. She had written faithfully during his sojourn in the infirmary, at first begging mercifully to be at his side, then acceding to his admonition that "this is no town at present for a beautiful young lady to be unescorted . . . there are toughs and toughs constantly about, using war-time as an excuse to raise hell." She wrote back that she understood his concern and loved him all the more for it and "while I will abide your feelings for my welfare, I shall constantly pray that you will not despair in your own grief and discomfort."

How he longed to embrace her once more, to feel the firmness of her lips and to see the glow of love in her eyes! It wasn't easy, he told himself, to refuse to allow her to cut school and come down to Washington.

Even now, just a few hours away from being with her and the family back in Old Dorp, he was in no hurry to reach Albany. He dreaded to see the agony on Maggie Peissner's face.

* * * * * *

June 1, 1863 . . . "Arrived in Schenectady safely, and am now back among my loved ones. Poor Peissner has been put beneath the sod and the gentle rippling of the Hudson chants his requiem."

Upon arriving at the Albany port, Charles grabbed a bite to eat and then booked a four-horse Overland coach direct to Schenectady, arriving at South College just before dark.

His greeting was one of genuine warmth and cheerfulness, not the sort of gloom and doom he had expected. As he walked past the Blue Gate and on up to the steps of the Lewis apartment, Charles bit his lower lip in anticipation of a tearful scene. He set his duffle on the stone landing, then slowly opened the door.

Jane Keziah Lewis spotted him first. She was passing through the front corridor from the parlor, stood frozen and open-eyed for a moment. She cried, "It's my son! My son!" and ran to kiss him and throw her arms about his neck.

The others came running from the parlor where, apparently, they were waiting for his arrival. Charles had written that he might be home sometime that night. Professor Lewis, Maggie Peissner and her two children — Barbara "Babbitt" who was four-and-a-half, and Tayler Lewis Peissner who would be two on June 7 — all were wild with excitement and smothered the homecoming hero with kisses and hugs. They were most careful, however, not to touch his left arm. He winced once or twice despite their caution, but it was a joy to be home again.

Mother Lewis was most solicitous about the injury — whether it was still painful, how much it hurt, what the doctors said about it, and how long it might take to heal — all from which Charles backed off.

"Don't worry about it, Mother, the worst is over and I'll be on the mend . . . now that I'm home."

Babbitt kept looking at him and his crippled arm, her eyes hauntingly sad as she stood beside Maggie, clinging to her mother's black satin gown. Charles knew instinctively what her young mind was mulling over: "He was with my Daddy and he got that bad arm the same time my Daddy was killed." In effect, her Uncle Charles was something special because he and her father suffered together to the very end.

Charles also sensed that his sister was anxious to talk about her husband and all that happened at Chancellorsville, but prudently avoided any mention of it for now. And for that, he was grateful.

The professor got out his best Madeira for the occasion, and they had just toasted Charles's homecoming and recovery when the honored guest suddenly asked: "Where's Kate . . . didn't she say she would be here tonight?" He had written to her, too, and hoped that she would be at the family's house this night.

There was no explicit answer. Mother and Father Lewis looked at each other, then Maggie spoke up.

"We are not sure she could make it. There was something about extra school work, but she would hope to be here by the time you arrived. Don't worry Charles, she hasn't forgotten you . . . I would say she lives for you alone."

"I'm sure she does, but there must be something wrong to keep her away," he said, puzzled at the vague response to his query. "I've got to get down to her place and see her — now! If I should be a bit late, don't wait up for me . . . I'll find my old room all right, but it does take me time to get undressed these days."

The others looked after him as he went out, but said nothing. Once the door was closed, Mother Lewis shook her head.

"I hope he doesn't stay out too long. That boy has been very sick and he needs all the care and rest we can give him so he can be well again."

* * * * * *

The night was still young and the air stirred a new warmth into Charles as he strode smartly down the college terrace and turned down Liberty Street toward the Smith house. He wore the same clothes he painfully and slowly donned at the hospital early that morning, an officer's parade uniform of Union blue. If there had been time, he'd have bathed, shaved and put on fresh duds . . . but at this moment he felt an urgency to see Kate at all costs.

Was there something wrong? Why wasn't she at the house with the others?

He fairly bounded up the wood porch steps and turned the key of the old brass doorbell. In a moment there was the sound of heels clicking on the wooden hallway floor inside, and the door opened wide. There, dressed fetchingly in a "schoolmarm's uniform" of a dark blue full-length skirt and a white blouse with lace collar, stood Kate in all her beauty. Her eyes were widened with excitement, her mouth slightly open. Then her arms opened wide and she flung them around her lover's neck as they embraced and shared a kiss to make up for 10 months' absence.

Widow Smith was abed with ague, something her physician, Dr. Barent Mynderse, said was a "plague on older people", but Kate and Charles went to the bedroom and said a brief hello. The poor woman looked pale and thin, wrapped in bedclothes despite the warm weather, and she waved a weak greeting toward Charles while managing a wan smile.

Back to the sitting room, Kate explained that her mother's illness was the main reason she could not join the others at the Lewis House. They sat on a horsehair sofa, and he had gathered her slim waist in his good arm, kissing her tenderly about the lips, eyes and neck. She threw off her shoes, tucked her feet beneath her and snuggled against Charles' downturned head with a deep sigh.

"Oh Charles, my darling, you can never know just how much I've missed you, worried so about you all these months . . . and when we learned about the awful fight, Elias's death and your injury, I was about to go out of my mind! Thank the good Lord you're home now and I don't even want to think about your ever going back to that terrible war."

She and her family had recently mourned the loss of her younger brother, Maus, a few months before. He had been buried on the battlegrounds of Chantilly. She wrote of it once in a letter and never mentioned it again; nor did she now. Kate also told him about Peissner's funeral service at the college chapel. She had been there with the family but did not join them at dinner later.

"It was a most touching ritual, Charles," she said. "Maggie bore up well, her children beside her. She was braver than I could ever have been."

As he walked slowly, thoughtfully, back to the campus dwelling several hours later, Charles was a bit befuddled.

It was a joyous homecoming. His family outdid the welcome to the prodigal son. Kate was warmer, closer to him than ever. A wonderful evening all around, he thought . . . but was it really a sick mother who kept Kate away from South College?

* * * * * *

The young captain lost no time the following day in calling on Hattie Potter. She was young, probably just past her teens. Her face was more angular than round and, despite her sober intense features, she was a good-looking woman. Her straw-colored hair was parted in the middle and combed tightly back. Hattie wore plain black. Most of the women in Schenectady wore black, or so it seemed.

Charles told her about Henry Schwerin before the battle of Chancellorsville, his coolness under fire and in facing death. She smiled for the first time when he mentioned the trinkets and the packet of letters he was unable to salvage for her.

"It's best, Captain," she said quietly. "I'm pleased that he kept them. His memory will be my richest treasure, and what you have told me today makes it even more precious. I know this hasn't been easy for you, your own grief and all, and I want you to know I'll always be grateful."

Charles admired her calm composure as she strained to hide her sorrow. She would have made Henry Schwerin a good wife. As the heavy oak door at 4 Union Street closed behind him, he could hear her sobbing.

The morning sun slanted through the maples along the lower avenue, touching them like a spotlight, and he stopped for a moment in front of the nearly completed First Reformed Church to admire its magnificence. Basking in the sunlight, its beautiful steeple and weather vane fairly glowed.*

His arm ached beneath the sling his sister had fixed for him, but he was thinking now of Henry Schwerin and Hattie Potter, Joe and Jonas Carter, of Elias Peissner and Maggie, Maus Smith, and comrades of Company C.

"A strange world, this. We seem to grow stronger after sorrow. I can feel it now, after my first experience on the battlefield. Not so much putting our trust in the Lord . . . but strength after sorrow."

He spoke of this after dinner that night, and his father listened intently.

"Wherever you go, whatever you do, my son," Professor Lewis told him, "never lose this faith. It will see you through the darkest hour and you will be stronger for it. Remember what the Good Book tells us: 'He will swallow up death in victory; and the Lord God will wipe away tears from all faces'."

*See "Burning of the Church" page 142.

The "seat of stone" (at left) on the college terrace, where Charles had his chat with Dr. Eliphalet Nott. South College (nearest camera) and North College buildings are in center background.

Chapter 6
A Talk With Dr. Nott

> *June 4, 1863 . . . "I was honored today to have Dr. Nott among my several visitors who came to wish me well. I fear he has not long to be among the living, but what an extraordinary legacy he has left not only our college but many hundreds of boys who have gone on to greater heights because of his lofty ideals."*

These first few days at home, a number of people from campus and in town came by to visit the recuperating soldier, and one of the first was Dr. Eliphalet Nott, Union's esteemed president.

Charles sat upright from his half-sprawled position on the limestone wall, the "seat of stone" which bridged the college terrace from Blue Gate to North Gate, Union Street to Nott Street. He had just seen the dignified old man leave the veranda of the prexy's house and start walking toward him.

Doctor Nott wore his high-necked black waistcoat and, despite the warm weather, a cape was thrown about his shoulders, His glossy silk hat was as much a part of him as the highly polished walking stick which tapped the stone walk as he took slow, mincing steps along the terrace.

They had a pleasant conversation, although the young officer was inwardly disturbed over the great change, mentally and physically, that had come over Doctor Nott in the past two years.

Just the day before, Tayler Lewis mentioned the fact that Nott would become 90 on June 25, at which time the faculty would honor him at dinner on campus.

"He may be old," Doctor Lewis said, "but he is still the strong guiding hand and bulwark of respectability that has made Union one of the leading colleges of this country."

He had been the young minister of Albany's First Presbyterian Church when he took over Union's presidency in 1804. Publication of a sermon against dueling, inspired by the tragic death of Alexander Hamilton, had won him considerable attention. Union College's fortunes soared to unprecedented heights and much of it was attributed to the new president's rare vision and shrewd business sense.

Charles had heard his father tell of the educator's great reputation for handling "unmanageable" youths. One of these "bad boys" was William H. Seward, Class of 1820, who left the campus and journeyed, hobo style, down to Georgia. The Auburn lad was reclaimed by Doctor Nott, under whose counsel Seward began to develop those qualities which enabled him to become New York State governor, senator and first choice in Lincoln's cabinet after losing the Republican presidential nomination in 1860.

His "boys", as he referred to anyone who ever attended Union, were the doctor's chief concern. Perhaps it was this, rather than advancing age, that had now caused the old man's speech to falter and his every movement to become feeble.

Only three years before, the Class of 1860 — then largest graduating class in Union's 65 year history — heard Doctor Nott proclaim "the joy that is mine today in the making of so many useful citizens". Union had always been a popular college with the South and nearly every southern state was represented among Minerva's undergraduates.

The following year, however, wrought the changes which Charles saw reflected in the aged administrator's ashen, wrinkled features as he sat beside him on the stone wall.

"The bitterness that is in men's hearts will be erased by time, my boy," the old man remarked sadly, punctuating his words by the soft tapping of his walking stick. "The sons of many of my boys who left here — no matter what side their fathers fought on — will come to Union to study, and there will be an even stronger bond between them."

He paused a moment, reflecting upon what he had just said.

"I would like nothing better than to be here when that day comes, but my time is growing short. All that remains for me, my boy, is to savor the firm conviction that it will come true."

He rose with an effort, finally regaining his feet. He patted Charles on the shoulder, tipped his hat and continued his morning's constitutional down the terrace.

Charles would remember this meeting when, at the outset of 1866, he heard of Doctor Nott's death and burial in the Vale. And also, within ten years, when Dr. Eliphalet Nott Potter would restore to the college the patronage of southern students — just as his grandfather had predicted.

* * * * * *

The next day, a Friday, Charles walked downtown to buy tickets for that night's stage performance at Anthony Hall. He, Kate, Mother and Father Lewis agreed it would be a pleasant diversion and the play, "Richard III", was the rage of that season.

He picked up the tickets in Bill Anthony's saloon-restaurant at Ferry and Liberty Streets, then walked around the corner to get a haircut at John Hardy's shop, two doors below the Barney store. A red-and-white striped barber pole hung out beside the second floor window where Hardy's one-room tonsorial palace was located. Charles, a frequent customer here in recent years, was greeted heartily by the shop owner, who had been shaving a portly gentleman tilted back horizontally on the chair like a beached whale.

"Charley Lewis, as I live and breathe," the slight-built man gushed, shaking the other's good hand long and hard. "It's been so long since you've been up here . . . but I heard about you being away in the army, your injury and all. And poor Professor Peissner . . . isn't it awful, this killing and our poor country torn to bits? Why we oughta bring them all home and let the generals settle it!"

Hardy was one of the few people to call him Charley, even though the captain preferred his proper Christian name, but Charles never made an issue of it. He was the friendly type, a bit talkative but it helped pass the time while in the chair. However, the barber's cavalier attitude about the war galled Charles, whose dark scowl as he went to sit down by the window was sufficient to send Hardy back to his shaving.

"I'm sorry, Charley, if I misspoke myself," he apologized. "I guess us civvies have a lot to learn."

"War is hell any way you look at it, John. Every last one of us in the field, North or South, would lay down our guns and shake hands in a minute if a solution could be found to settle the differences. But until that happens, each of us must fight to the bitter end for what he believes . . . we know it, but the people at home have other ideas. Now I've had my say, John, and I'd just as soon let it lay."

Another five minutes and John had finished. The big man climbed out of the chair, ambled over to the counter and mirror where he splashed on witch hazel and combed his reddish brown sideburns, mustache and wispy hair. He turned toward Charles, now in the barber's chair with a towel around his shoulders.

"Heard what you said awhile ago, young fellow," he said, now hooking thumbs back of his bright red suspenders, emphasizing his tremendous girth. "And what you say makes a good deal of sense. We've got a lot to learn here at home from you boys who have been in the fight. Why, if I were just a few years younger, I'd be right out there with the rest of you, believe me . . . but all I can do is what any ordinary citizen should try to do — tighten his belt until it hurts!"

Then he turned and started down the stairs, which creaked under the heavy load. John stepped back, looked at Charles with the same incredulous stare, and they both burst into laughter.

* * * * * *

That night, the Lewises were driven by carriage down to Anthony Hall for the three-act play which began at 8 p.m. Kate had joined them for dinner at the house and now was more at ease sitting next to Charles in the theater.

It was a moderately sized auditorium, located on the second floor of Anthony's brick corner building, which was reached by a stairway entrance off Liberty Street. A string orchestra seated in front of the stage provided soft music before curtain time and between the acts.

The performance was above reproach, although they thought veteran actor Douglas Forrest ranted and raved to excess. A young actress, Miss Annie Waite, was well received by the full house of some 300 persons and happily accepted three large bouquets at curtain call. Professor Lewis remarked that he had seen her in a performance at the Gayety Theatre in Albany early in 1861 while attending a statewide convention at the capital. She had the role of Portia in "The Merchant of Venice", while portraying the part of Shylock was the budding actor, John Wilkes Booth.

Dr. Eliphalet Nott

Chapter 7
Kate's Classroom

June 8, 1863... "All have been so good to me and have shown such a love for me. Nothing has been too good or precious, and the fatted calf has been daily, hourly killed."

He had been home a week when Charles began pleading that he would become an invalid if he were not allowed to do anything but lie back among the soft pillows of the parlor couch or sit on the front steps and bask in the sun.

If his "broken wing" was on the mend, it was taking its own time and already he was getting restless. It ached still and sudden movements, especially when he was asleep in bed, sent stabbing pain through his shoulder and neck.

"Hell, it's been over a month," Charles mumbled as he got up that morning, carefully rubbing the arm strapped to his side. "Bones can be mighty fragile things for something under cover!"

He was scheduled for an appointment at 10 a.m. with the family doctor, Dr. Alexander G. Fonda, whose office was at 13 Union Street just below the Dutch church. He would examine the arm and tissue to see how the wound was healing, afterward cleaning and dressing the broken skin. The cool brownish salve, which smelled like tar, felt soothing as the doctor spread it gingerly over the darkened scab.

"It's coming along nicely, Charles," Doc Fonda said cheerfully as he wrapped fresh gauze about the wound. "In another month, you should be as good as new. . .well, almost. Come in and see me next week."

At home, Mother Lewis waited on him constantly and his father, wrapping up his classes in a shortened semester, spent most of his spare hours with his son, discussing theology, war and politics in general. Charles did get away, occasionally walking downtown to watch the boats glide under the canal bridges or to sit on a station platform bench to see the trains come and go, people boarding or departing. It was busier than he ever remembered it. The sidewalks, especially west of the canal, were crowded with shoppers and the cobblestone streets were well used by horsedrawn equipment of all kinds, many of them tethered to the hitching posts at curbside.

He always enjoyed going for long rides, either on horseback or carriage, but now he didn't feel up to it. Riding horseback was out. Too many bumps and jars, and he couldn't manage with just one arm. On this day, however, after visiting the doctor, walking around downtown, having lunch with the family, and lolling outside in the shade of a lofty elm, Charles had an idea.

He had been thinking of Kate, what she might be doing up at the school, when the thought struck him: "What if I drove up there to see her. . .wouldn't she be surprised!" He got permission to use the family buggy but to "be careful and not overexert yourself."

Horses and rigs for faculty were kept in a carriage house beside the gymnasium, a facility maintained by a liveryman named Moses Viney. The story was that Moses and two other slaves escaped from bondage in the South some 20 years before the war, aided by the Underground Railroad, and later he was hired by Dr. Eliphalet Nott as driver/footman on Union College's campus.

Charles had always enjoyed talking to Moses, even when a boy in short pants, because the black man was a jovial sort with a giggling kind of laugh. Nothing ever seemed to bother him and he enjoyed the livery work and being around people.

Moses had brought around the professor's gig, pulled by old Bill, a chestnut brown, and now Charles headed out the main gate and turned east toward the Niskayuna Turnpike. There were only a few homes beyond Nott Terrace and most of these were farmhouses. The campus itself sprawled north of Union Street, bordered roughly by Union Street, Park Place, Nott Street and Wendell Avenue, and most of this was wooded land nurtured by Hans Groote Kill.

Usually, Kate paid a small weekly sum to Francis Calo, railroad baggage agent, to ride with him on the front seat of his platform spring wagon as he made his early morning deliveries uptown. If she couldn't hitch a ride back to the city with a friendly Niskayuna family, Kate walked out to the Troy Road and waited for a passenger coach to come by via Latham.

Niskayuna P.S. 35 schoolhouse was small, built of weatherbeaten clapboards and battens which could use some paint. As Charles drove up to it, he purposely slowed Bill to a walk and checked the time. The gold watch, which had come through hails of bullets, told him it was 2 p.m. — a half hour before school closing. He parked the rig under some shade trees and walked across to the schoolground. It wore a fringe of green grass around the sides, the center of which was as smooth as a ballroom floor from the playing of tiny bare feet. It was enclosed by a plain board fence, an ideal backstop for hard clay marbles.

He hadn't planned it, but suddenly he decided to go inside. It would be interesting to watch how Kate, timid little Kate, managed to teach so many children of all ages and still keep a semblance of order.

Behind the front door was a small vestibule. A rope hung down an opening which led up to the small bell in a roof cupola. A water pail was on a stool and a tin dipper hung beside it. There was a row of nails in the entrance hall for hats and coats, but none were needed this day.

Kate was seated behind a huge flat-top desk at the other end of the schoolroom, facing more than two dozen pupils whose ages appeared to range from six to sixteen. A pot-bellied wood stove stood alone in the middle of the room. The class would gather around it for warmth during the winter. It was useful also in other months for sharpening slate pencils and for Kate to empty the dust pan when she swept out in the morning before classes began.

Every head turned as the uniformed visitor walked in, saw a vacant wood stool in a far corner and went over to sit on it. Kate had nodded politely his way but as her guest sat down, the whole room erupted with snickers and laughter. Kate clapped her hands twice and restored order.

"Class, this is my fiance, Capt. Charles F. Lewis of the 119th New York. He is home on leave, recuperating from a battle wound. Now, people, I am sure you will all forgive him for sitting in the dunce chair, it being the only one available at the time. I am just as certain you can understand, too, that even a war hero may be embarrassed, as the Captain is right now. Now that we have welcomed him, let's get back to our lessons. Eyes front, everybody!"

Charles was utterly shocked, and he told her so afterward, at his beloved's cool demeanor in the classroom. She allowed a certain amount of talking and whispering during lessons, because she could teach only one group at a time while the others had to go about their own classwork. . .but if it got a bit out of hand, she had only to clap her hands twice, briskly, and there was dead silence. She was friendly but serious in her manner of teaching, Charles thought, and those kids of all ages responded in kind.

The last pupil hardly had whooped out the door, when Kate had gathered a few books and personal effects, locked the windows and stepped to the front door, key in hand. She paused, looked up at her lover's serious countenance, and tip-toed to give him a peck on the cheek.

"What a most pleasant surprise, my dear Captain. . .I wish all my schooldays could end this way! But do tell, what really prompted this visit? Was it to see if I could conduct classes or just because you've missed me so?"

"Actually, my sweet, it was both of those reasons," Charles said, now smiling but in all earnestness. "You've opened my eyes to a different side of you. Here I've been thinking you are a soft, lovable, adorable female, not in the least given to deceiving the stronger sex. But from what I've seen this afternoon, you could keep a platoon in line a darn sight slicker than some of the misfits we have in command!"

Kate smiled back, and squeezed his hand as they walked across the road to the buggy.

"Ah, now you must beware. If women are to be regarded as the weaker sex, they must also be given the courtesy of choosing their weapons in life's unending battle. If it be brawn or brains, my choice will be the latter — every time."

In the buggy, he lifted his right arm and put it around her, managing to hold the reins in his good hand. She leaned against him, and neither said a word for several miles as old Bill clip-clopped down Niskayuna Road. At times like this, silence really *was* golden.

49

Prof. Tayler Lewis

Jane Keziah Lewis

Margaret Peissner with daughter Babbitt

Tayler Lewis Jr.

Chapter 8
A Sister's Concern

> *June 11, 1863 ... "Dear sister Maggie is a rarity. Half of her life virtually was wiped out in one fell swoop, yet she carries on with dignity, uncomplaining but concerned for the welfare of others. There will be a special place in Heaven for her when it comes time to join her beloved."*

This Thursday mid-morning, Charles got the carriage from the livery and drove down to Maggie's house just below the college on Union Street. It was a summery day, sunny bright and a slight warming breeze, perfect for one they had chosen for a ride and "a talk".

His sister had the children all ready for their visit at the Lewis home, prearranged so the two adults could speak more freely. Babbit and Tayler were bubbling with excitement because Grandmother Lewis had promised to go on a picnic up in the woods in the east sector of the campus.

As they drove down Nott Street toward Maxon Road and Volney Freeman's toll bridge, Charles and Maggie indulged in pleasantries and light conversation. Once across the bridge and past the toll booth, on up toward East Glenville, Maggie's demeanor began to change. Dressed in widow's black, as she had since May 8th when she received word of her husband's death, her face seemed to stiffen as she touched her brother's hand — the one holding the reins. Tears welled up in her eyes and when the words finally came, she spoke them softly, hesitatingly.

"Charles, I confess to wanting to talk to you about Elias as the real reason for asking for this time alone with you . . . I hope you will understand, knowing in my heart it must not be pleasant for you to talk about it . . . but I have been tormented so these last few weeks, wondering about Elias. He wrote often but I'm sure he didn't tell me everything, how he liked the army life and the men, if he got along with everyone . . . if there were times when he might have talked to you about death . . . if, God forbid, he might have faced it with any feeling of regret that he ever came to this country, that he might have stayed in Germany and had a family there. Oh Charles, tell me truly, was there ever such a time?"

Plainly, his sister had been under tremendous emotional stress during the past month, trying to accept her husband's sudden demise and to pacify the children, and now harboring doubts as to whether Elias had been content with his role as an American soldier and father.

Charles was silent a few minutes as he pulled old Bill over to the side of the dusty, dirt road leading to Alplaus village. Then he turned to Maggie, placed his hand atop both of hers, clasped in her lap.

"Sis, I don't know where to begin but I do know that you deserve to hear all that I may find it in my power to remember about Elias while we were in the field together, the things we said . . . even confided to each other . . . but most of all, his feelings toward you and about the children.

"Believe me, Maggie, there isn't the slightest doubt that Elias considered himself the most fortunate man alive for having come to America. He loved freedom so much he was ready to lay down his life for it, and that he did. That alone was not his greatest joy, however . . . it was meeting you, loving you, having a family and being with all of us here in Schenectady. He remarked about this many times over the past months, even on that night before we went into the big fight . . . He was a proud and happy man right to the end, Sis, and his most cherished possession was you."

Suddenly came to mind an incident of several years ago, in March of 1861, when he was invited to accompany Elias on a trip over to the village of Scotia.

"I remember that night so well, Maggie. I was still a novice, in my freshman year at Union and in awe of my illustrious brother-in-law . . . so I was flattered when he asked me to be his driver and escort. He was to speak at the Scotia Baptist church over in the settlement and when we got there, we were almighty surprised to find the building overflowing with people from both the village and city. Probably two hundred or more were there, all anxious to hear what Elias would say about Lincoln's problems that very month of his inauguration and, worse, the threat of war between the states.

"Maggie, he was wonderful. He held the people spellbound, myself included, but he finished up with a message of hope in the future of our country . . . no matter what might happen if a rebellion took place. Everyone shook his hand, patted him on the back and asked him to come back again. I tell you, I was real proud of him that night.

"But what I want most to tell you about that night was what he told me as we were driving back across the covered bridge. He said there were three more days until the fourth anniversary of the most important day in his life . . . the day you two were married in the chapel. That's how he felt about you Maggie, my girl!"

Maggie sighed heavily and looked at Charles with shining, grateful eyes as she daubed at them with a lacy hanky. Then, as her brother continued to reminisce, she held his hand tightly between hers and put her head on his shoulder.

He told her more than he had ever expected to, mostly about Elias . . . their ride down to Washington with the recruits and their many talks together, the stalled encampments, the drudgery of winter quarters, the meals they ate, some of the oddballs in service, the southern farms and people encountered on marches, seeing the enemy across river while on picket duty and waving at each other.

He told her about the fight at Chancellorsville, the mistakes that had been made by command, and — ultimately — going into battle and seeing Elias fall with many of his comrades. He told her about that awful moment as gently as possible, without purposely omitting details of the incident, knowing she would never have peace of mind otherwise.

"Elias died a hero if ever there was one, Maggie," Charles concluded, after a brief pause to catch his breath. "He was an inspiration to all who knew him and saw him fight to the last against overwhelming odds. You, all of us, can be proud of him always."

He had talked long enough, but was grateful for having said all that he did. And when Maggie reached over and kissed him full on the lips, he felt a great burden had been lifted from his shoulders.

It was a happier Maggie who sat beside Charles as he snapped the reins briskly to start up again. As they passed under the beautiful maple trees lining the main drive through Alplaus, she commented without remorse that it reminded her of the road leading to the cemetery in Fort Miller.

"It's a lovely place, Charles . . . so peaceful and picturesque. You must get up to see it before your leave is over. Elias would like that."

They continued at a slow pace down through Rexford, past Cyrus Rexford's general store and Mickey Travis's restaurant opposite the canal lock. After paying toll and crossing the vehicular bridge beside the aqueduct, Charles pulled the rig over to one side so they could stretch their legs and admire the view.

It was like old times for both of them, sitting on the hillside at the tiny settlement of Craig, looking down at the Erie Canal winding its way northward toward the aqueduct which crossed the Mohawk into Rexford on the opposite end. As children, they were brought here many times as a favorite family excursion, mostly on weekends when the weather was as balmy as it was today. They watched the drivers and their mules and horses, trudging along the towpath as the barges moved slowly in back of them, finally reaching the great aqueduct — a trough of water atop a bridge built on huge stone arches. In the distance, lock tenders readied the gates for the lock-through. The sound of their coarse voices, filtering clear across the river, punctured the stillness around them.

Finally, they walked back to the carriage. Charles patted old Bill's head, stroked his mane while stepping around to help Maggie to her seat.

"Time to get back, I guess, Sis. It's been an afternoon to remember, hasn't it? A lot has been said that needed saying and, as for me, I feel much better having spent these hours with you . . . just as we used to."

Maggie agreed, heartily, but broached another subject.

"Charles, there's one more thing we should discuss openly while we are in this frame of mind. It has to do with Kate. You must have sensed a certain strained relationship between her and the family . . . and I feel I must take the initiative to give you our side of it.

"Kate is an adorable person, Charles, and some day will make you a wonderful wife . . . but you are both so young and you still must complete your education, find your life's work, before taking your vows. Mother and Father have taken a stronger stand on this than I, but to be honest, I do agree with their logic. Kate has, more or less, intimated that you two will be wed very soon.

"Please, dear brother, think hard on this before you take a step which may ruin your life and hers. We love you both and wish you every happiess . . . but there comes a time when common sense must be obeyed by every one of us."

So now it was in the open. Charles sucked in a deep breath as he sat silently beside his sister, pondering every sobering word she had uttered. He had, indeed, perceived a growing schism between his betrothed and his family but not, until now, had he known of its cause.

"Frankly, Sis, I am at a loss of words after what you've just told me," he said. "I do appreciate your concern for my future, yours and the family, but I'm of a mind to say that whatever Kate and I decide is our decision alone. We love each other, that we know, and plan to spend the rest of our lives together. Whether we start now or a few years later, seems to be something which concerns only the two of us."

As the carriage bumped along the river road leading to Maxon Road and the college grounds, few words were exchanged between the siblings who had spent a full afternoon in frank discussion.

* * * * * *

July 30, 1863 . . . "Kate and I had a nice day together. Now that my arm is no longer painful, I think perhaps my disposition also may have improved but feeling better reminds me that my time here at home is rapidly growing short. It is like pulling teeth just to think of leaving dear Kate and everyone here at home."

The pain was gone and he no longer needed a sling for his wounded left arm, but Charles was becoming aware that for the rest of his life he could not use it naturally. It would not raise above his shoulder and he could not keep it comfortably at his side; rather he found it more convenient to hold the elbow outward, arm akimbo.

"Don't fret, my darling," Kate smiled. "As long as you can put both arms around me, we shan't notice the difference."

They were on an outing this Monday mid-morning, heading out the old river road toward Rotterdam's Woestyne. It was one of many memorable times they had together for the past six weeks, as many as Charles could fit into his remaining furlough without slighting the family. And because he was on the move so often, he declined the use of the family carriage, instead renting a rig from Bill Pettingill's livery on State Street just east of the railroad tracks.

He had called on Kate once more up at her school in late June, It being her last day that semester, and they took a long ride throughout the Niskayuna

The falls at Platte Kill

back roads east of Balltown Road. The view from one rocky bluff, overlooking the shale cliffs beyond and the gently flowing river below, was spectacular. On the way back, they stopped at the farm residence of George Leman, one of the school trustees, to leave the schoolhouse key to his safekeeping. He was a jolly, round-faced fellow with jet-black hair and a curled mustache he was fond of twirling. He insisted they stay for lunch before returning to Schenectady.

They had been invited to dinner one night at Maggie's, twice at the Lewis house, and went one night to eat at the Hotel Givens' ancient but intimate dining room with its candlelit tables and silver service. Kate also cooked several meals for them at her house, the widow Smith dining with them although in obvious discomfort. In less than a year, Kate would write that her mother's battle with infirmity was over and now both parents were gone.

They also had a serious talk about marital plans. Charles said nothing about his discussion with Maggie, but stood by his vow that they should be married "whenever we feel in our hearts that the time is right". And Kate, bless her, had promised she would do her utmost to avoid family discord on that subject.

Charles could handle the reins with either hand now, so it was even more comforting to have Kate snuggled close and his right arm fully about her as the two-wheeled buggy bounced merrily along the river road. It was muddy and rutted in some spots due to a recent rain, but this day was sunny and promised to be a scorcher by early afternoon. They rode at a moderate pace out past Schermerhorn Road and alongside the canal, waving a few times at boaters and their families.

In a few miles they came to the Platte Kill (which some people called Plotterkill) and it was here that Charles turned the rig inward toward a small grove beside the road. They alighted and, after securing the horse and leaving it under heavy shade, began a walk along a small pathway leading toward hilly country. Wildflowers abounded — bull thistle, daisies, purple cowslips, devil's paintbrush and red fireweed in profusion — and their sweet smell gave nature's welcome to two young lovers on a summer's picnic.

Kate had fixed a lunch in a wicker basket, and this Charles toted along as they slowly picked their way along a path which led to the spot where picnickers usually headed. This was a picturesque setting, just a half mile in from the road yet breathtaking to a newcomer. Kate was one of these, and her eyes shone with wonder at the enchantment of the scene before them.

The clean waters of the Platte Kill tumbled down four tiers of dark clay rock jutting out from a background of fern, flowering shrubs and indigenous trees. The step-like falls glistened in shafts of sunlight, ending in a pool that swirled and fed the creek which continued its course down to the river.

Charles had been here a number of times, both with his family and school chums, but somehow Platte Kill never looked as eye-catching as it did this day. He and Kate strolled hand-in-hand around the base of the falls, then came back to sit on a shale boulder — far enough removed so they could take in the beauty of the whole setting. This is where, afterward, they ate the picnic lunch and quite thoroughly enjoyed the other's company.

* * * * * *

In the post that evening, Charles had received a letter from Col. Allen H. Jackson, a Schenectady man from the 134th New York, commenting on the departure of General Hooker, who was relieved of command of the Army of the Potomac on orders of President Lincoln and replaced by Maj. Gen. George G. Meade, effective June 28.

He had read of it in the Evening Star, but Charles was further disturbed at the news while reading Jackson's letter.

Apparently, much blame was laid to Hooker's command because of the ill-fated Chancellorsville episode. According to Jackson, Hooker wanted to counter by marching south to capture Richmond while Lee was going north, but the military brass in Washington vetoed that for fear the capital would fall prey to Lee's forces.

"Hooker is the kind of leader we must have to help bring all this to a close," Charles told his father. "I do hope Lincoln will relent and find a place for him . . . Our fighting generals are scarce as it is."

Jackson said that Hooker wrote a farewell address to his troops at Frederick, Md., before boarding a spring wagon for the Frederick railroad station on his way to Baltimore to await further orders.

"I don't think we've seen the last of Fightin' Joe," Jackson remarked in his letter. Neither did Charles.

Col. Allen H. Jackson

John DeBois' photographic studio was on second floor of this building, located on east corner of State and South Ferry Streets. (DeBois can be seen peering from third window from left) where Charles and sister Maggie had their picture taken on August 4, 1863. The print of one of the poses is shown in insert.

Chapter 9
Furlough Ending

August 4, 1863 ... "The weather is oppressively hot. Tomorrow my leave expires; my arm is well healed and I return to the Army."

Charles and his sister rode downtown in the family carriage, and he tied the horse to a hitching post in front of E.L. Freeman's paint store near the corner of State and South Ferry streets.

It had been Maggie's idea that they have a photograph made together, so they walked upstairs to the studio of John DeBois, who advertised "the cheapest and best work done in the city." DeBois, a short, slender fellow with a nervous twitch to the left side of his face, seemed just as skittish setting up his bulky equipment and getting his subjects posed beneath dust-laden skylights.

He made several exposures of them, singly and together. Each time DeBois had carefully fitted the metal immobilizer back of their head, he called out, "Steady now . . . don't move!", as he held the lens cap in one hand and a stop watch in the other. It was an exposure of one minute. Standing absolutely still for that amount of time, without blinking or swallowing, was no mean feat. Some men used the trick of inserting a hand inside a partially unbuttoned coat to steady their pose. DeBois bragged that his film emulsion was nearly a minute faster than most in the area.

When it was over, the photographer promised Maggie he'd have prints ready the following week. A year before, Charles recalled, he and Elias came here to be photographed in their newly tailored uniforms and gave DeBois fits when they insisted the glass plates be developed the same day "lest the glamor wears off."

Humid air had closed in about the city that day, but business downtown seemed unaffected. It was well after ten and every store was open, most of them having already set up sidewalk displays. There were dozens of shoppers walking about on both sides of the street, many of the ladies toting parasols to shade them from the sun. Several uniformed men, mostly army privates, were among the pedestrians and Charles acknowledged the salutes as they passed by.

Charles and Maggie meandered from store to store, more or less passing the time and enjoying each other's company before returning home. She could not be at the farewell dinner this night and she already told him she could not bear to see him off the next day, so this was to be their last time together — for how long, neither knew.

In the window of Young & Graham's stationery shop, a few doors up from H.S. Barney's, was a display of current sheet music "for piano or guitar accompaniment". Most were war or patriotic songs, selling for 30 cents a copy. One was titled "Mother Kissed Me in My Dream", a song based on the Battle of Antietam. Another was "Kind Friends Are Near Her", which was an answer to "Who Will Care for Mother Now?" The biggest seller was the flag waver, "Hail, Glorious Banner of Our Land".

As they walked back toward the rig, a stagecoach was about to leave from in front of the Merchant's Hotel, just the other side of Ferry Street. Lackeys were hauling out trunks and suitcases, securing them in the rear storage rack and atop the four-horse coach. Amid a flurry of ruffles and petticoats, a pretty miss hurried from the hotel and boarded the vehicle as many an eye turned to catch a glimpse of a pair of shapely ankles.

"Now, now, Captain Lewis, eyes front," Maggie chided as her brother breathed a soft whistle. "I venture you're every bit the Casanova away from home . . . Kate had best nail you down at the first opportunity."

Charles grinned, and agreed with her.

* * * * * *

August 5, 1863... "This has been my last day home. At 7 p.m. left Old Durip and all its pleasures once more to 'jine the Army'. Kate, Father and many friends were at the depot to see me off. Father kissed me and I bade a fond farewell to my one and only. Time alone will tell when we are together once more."

When he arrived in New York late that night, Charles found it partially under martial law. Soldiers were picketed in a number of midtown sectors and allowed no movement of pedestrians or carriages after 8 p.m. except by official pass. Several buildings were scorched and debris lay in piles where it had been swept off the streets. This was the aftermath of the anti-draft riots in the big city just three weeks before, in which angry mobs overpowered the police, beat or killed blacks, and set fire to shops after looting them. One of the soldiers told Charles that order had been restored but "it will be some time before this city gets back its respectability after what went on here."

He stayed overnight in a downtown tourist house, then made it a point the next morning to visit Col. John Lockman, a friend of the 2nd Corps, at his uptown home. Lockman had written Charles in mid-July to tell him he had been wounded at Gettysburg and would be laid up for about a month. The man was in good spirits, Charles thought, and credited it to the fact that he was not injured severely and that the North considered Gettysburg a victory. At least Lee, Longstreet and Ewell could not break Union lines and were finally chased out of Federal country, back to Virginia and beyond.

Before leaving to entrain for Washington, Charles shook Lockman's hand and said they'd probably meet again soon, "farther South".

"You can bet on that, Lewis, and now that Vicksburg has fallen, we should begin to make some inroads," said Lockman. "This Gettysburg set-to may keep the Rebs out of Pennsylvania for good and give our troops greater latitude to force them deeper into pockets. Oh, by the way, Lewis, you may be interested to know that old (Maj. Gen. O.O.) Howard performed quite well at Gettysburg. He fell back at Round Top, but his troops rallied and helped win the day."

"Good for him, I'm glad for him," said Charles as he departed. But to himself, he murmured, "If only he had enjoyed such good luck at Chancellorsville."

* * * * * *

Once in Washington, Charles went to Carver Hospital where he was thoroughly checked over and found to be "ready for field duty, but be cautious of overly exerting the bad arm." He was given a signed medical release and now would take a horse cab over to the military general's office to obtain a pass through the lines to Catlett Station in Virginia, some 30 miles southwest of D.C.

This was where he was informed his regiment and the 11th Corps were quartered, awaiting deployment to another campaign area. Only now it was attached to the Army of the Cumberland and was "ready to move." Charles was pleased to hear this. Routine picket duty and lolling around camp was not doing much to putting a clincher to forcing surrender. Talk around the military office was that the Rebs were in bad shape and on the run, without adequate rations, clothing and ammunition.

Charles ate lunch at a nearby cafe before reporting back to the army center where he was to get transportation via military wagon to Catlett Station. However, on arrival there he found that the corps had already moved out to Brentsville, about 11 miles distant. Quartermaster clerk Jack Christy was the only one in the erstwhile campsite, now devoid of everything except a baggage wagon and two horses.

"Yes sir, they pulled out two days ago, Captain . . . I was told to stay here because you were due in. Mighty glad to see you, sir, and that your arm is better," the corporal told him.

Luckily, there were vittles in the wagon because it was too late to join the corps. He and Christy enjoyed a hot meal of beans and bacon, with sourdough and peaches to top it off. Then it began to rain, a real downpour. The wagon had no cover, so the two of them slept that night beneath it. Charles was pleased, though thoroughly drenched by morning, that his arm withstood the exposure without discomfort.

Joseph Hooker, the "fightin' General"

Chapter 10
Nashville Bound

September 18, 1863 ... "Terrific rainstorm all day, drenched to the skin. These are the days when there is no fun in soldiering. Am on railroad guard and have my force stretched all along the road from Bealton to the river. Moore brought me a letter this morning and received in it a tooth brush I had left at home. The economy and exactness of a mother is something remarkable."

The days following his reunion with the corps were not entirely eventful. Charles was on guard duty, court martial review and even assumed command as field officer on several occasions as Major Willis was "on a tear with the booze and exhibiting himself very prettily as a field officer."

There was constant moving about to Manassas Junction, back to Catlett Station, Martinsburg in West Virginia, until late September when marching orders indicated the corps was to go to the relief of the Western Army at Chattanooga, Tennessee. It was rumored that Longstreet's division had already left Lee's army in Virginia for the same part of the country.

The only war-related incident, as far as Charles was concerned, was the night of September 23 while doing his rounds at Rappahannock Station. He was shot at by a "sneaking bushwacker" in the dark. The bullet struck his sword scabbard, and did no injury except slightly laming his leg against which the scabbard was resting.

Finally, the 11th and 12th Corps, commanded by General Hooker, late of the Army of the Potomac, set out on a roundabout railroad trip to Tennessee by way of West Virginia, Ohio, Indiana and Kentucky. It was a secret move conceived by Secretary of War Edwin Stanton and his staff. The men were on half-rations for several days at a time, interspersed with camp duty and full mess kits.

At last, they settled into Nashville midst rain, sleet and wind, as miserable a setting as one might imagine while on picket duty the whole night. It went on for days, the rain and duty, and company morale began to match the dreariness. In his diary October 15, after writing letters to Kate and the family, Charles noted: "Another terrible thunderstorm in the night. This is great country we have struck, where everything seems 'sort of upside down like'."

Lt. John Lloyd and Lt. Arnold Hall had become his closest friends in the regiment; especially Lloyd, a self-effaced individual in his mid-thirties whom Charles had come to regard as an older brother. Lloyd was tough as nails, built solidly, and square-jawed to match the image of a man who could take care of himself — if needed. Lloyd was from New York City, and had left his young wife there two months before. Hall, who was single, matched Charles' age to the month, was slim, wiry and full of fun. He was a tonic in times like this. From one, Charles felt he could ask and get good advice on just about anything. From the other, he took solace in cheerful company.

On off-duty periods, the three visited other divisions in the encampment. Among them was the 61st Ohio, where they shared a few drinks and sandwiches with several of the officers while a driving rain pounded a relentless tattoo on the roof of the mess tent. One of them, a Major Tyndall, brought up an interesting subject.

"Helluva war this, isn't it? We're all down here fighting for what we believe is the true spirit of our nation — unity and freedom," he said. "But are we, really? The emancipation decree this year has freed the slaves, but are they free . . . like the rest of us? The coloreds have volunteered, regiments have been formed, and . . . unbeknown by most people in the North . . . they have already been in the thick of battle. And many of them are freed slaves."

The major paused to sip his scotch whiskey, wiped his lips, and went on.

"Yet, there is opposition in our states to having the coloreds in uniform. Why? One side of the whites think the coloreds can't fight while the other is afraid of their savagery! Do you know what, gentlemen? I think we here in the army should take a stronger stand in this matter. It's one thing to deny free men the right to fight for their country . . . and it's another thing for us to fight here and die without giving them that chance.

"I've got word that the War Department, even Lincoln himself, feels they must reassure citizens in the North that only white officers will be in charge of colored troops. Not only that, I hear there is a shortage of those officers simply because word hasn't been properly dispensed through channels.

"You can take this for what it's worth, but I for one am seriously considering making application for leadership of a colored unit. Not only would it be a promotion but a chance to leave this God-forsaken hole for more action. I've heard the coloreds are put into front lines right after basic training. Think about it . . . you'd get a promotion, an extended leave home, and then be in complete charge of men just panting to show they know how to fight as well or better than a white soldier!"*

Sloshing back to their tent, the three New Yorkers thought about Tyndall's remarks. It was something only vaguely familiar to them, another sore spot in this mixed-up war. Charles spoke up.

"Think he made any sense back there . . . Tyndall, I mean?"

"I can't say for sure I agree with his reasons to lead a colored regiment," said Lloyd, "but I sure as hell believe in his overall rationale as regards their being given the right to fight. Whether I'd ever qualify as a battalion commander is another thing."

On October 24, they moved camp eastward to Shellmunck and relieved the 26th Wisconsin, then on to Parson Valley two days later. Next stop, they were

*See "Civil War Potpourri" page 138.

told, was some 10 miles distant where the Rebs were well entrenched at Chattanooga and atop Lookout Mountain.

There was some shelling and skirmishes as the Confederates sought to stall the Federal advance. Charles was talking to Colonel Boughton of the 143rd New York at his headquarters when a large shell exploded some 20 feet away, wounding two soldiers standing in a group near them. When the blinding flash and explosion came, Charles thought he had been hit and it was a minute or two before he realized he had only been stunned.

Earlier that morning he had stumbled over a root, falling on his bad arm and hurting him quite badly. The pain persisted a few hours, then dissipated.

It had been a day to forget. He had hurt his arm, narrowly missed being bombed to oblivion, but . . . worse . . . he hadn't had any mail from home in nearly two weeks.

* * * * * *

November 20, 1863 . . . "Receiving this evening orders to march, it is thought the object of which will be to drive the Rebels from Lookout and Missionary Ridge. If that be our destination, God help us."

A general corps inspection was held the next morning by General Hooker, astride his black stallion and waving his slouch hat to the troops as he rode past the lines. Then they were ordered to move up the road toward Chattanooga, leaving baggage and camp equipment behind to be drawn up later by supply. It was determined that the wagons would have to make a detour of some 20 miles because of the deeply mired roads.

Gen. William Tecomseh Sherman had already pushed into Chattanooga, swinging around to form a north and west wing of the Union forces, with Thomas in the middle and Hooker on the right, at Lookout Valley. Meanwhile, Braxton Bragg, the Confederate cigar-chewing general, followed up his defeat of Gen. William S. "Wild Bill" Rosecrans at Chickamauga by taking up positions on Missionary Ridge and Lookout Mountain. From these heights, he was able to besiege the entire Army of the Cumberland.

In their tent city below the towering mountain, the men of the Cumberland began to be accustomed to the shelling from above, although most of it proved more a nuisance for its noise than a hazard to the troops. The Rebs also sent out sharpshooters, not for skirmish but for bushwacking at random. On picket duty one night, Charles had experienced some close calls — a bullet creasing his jacket and another zinging off the bark of a tree just above his head.

During one of his watches, he was visited by Colonel Jackson, the Union College cohort and commander of the 134th New York. The colonel was as brave as he was agreeable, but displayed such a brand of recklessness that many of his comrades doubted he would last through the war.

On this occasion, Charles was distressed to see the officer riding toward him. Jackson was mounted on his favorite black mare, seated on a big saddle with gold-embroidered cloth that extended from the withers to the croup of the handsome animal. Jackson wore light buckskin breeches and obviously had been imbibing commissary whiskey. Charles rose from his seat on a fallen tree to greet him, with the unpleasant feeling that they made a good mark for a Rebel sharpshooter.

Jackson had come down the line to chat about the latest news from home, seeing as how the mail had finally come in. But he didn't stay long. Before he was able to dismount, the crack of a rifle off to the right broke the silence. The colonel slid his right foot out of the stirrup and looked wide-eyed at a smooth crease across the top of his boot.

"By God, that was damned close!" he exclaimed. He kicked the mare's side and headed her down a gully of red clay which led back to camp.

One night, about ten, Confederate skirmishers made a bold attack on the left side of the picket line while Charles was in charge. The fire crept swiftly on until all save his extreme right was engaged. At times, the fire was hot and rapid, then would almost cease. It kept up for three hours or more, then the Rebels retired back up Lookout Mountain. In Charles' battalion, three men were slightly wounded, the most severe being a thumb that had to be amputated.

Two women, whose log house was in the line of fire a portion of the time, and in whose yard the picket reserve was drawn up, were terrified and at one point came running out screaming and with their hands to their ears. Charles advised them to stay in the cellar while the firing was going on, and they needed no urging. At daybreak, he called on them to come up out of the cellar, started a fire in the fireplace of the only room of the house, and chatted while warming themselves.

Later that day, after enjoying nearly 10 hours of unbroken sleep, Charles took out his packet of letters received a few days before. Some of them were two weeks old, but he read them as though he were talking to Kate, Father and Mother Lewis, Maggie and the children. His father had enclosed some novels and two copies of the Daily Times and Evening Star. Kate's several letters he devoured ravenously, just as he had done twice since their delivery.

One was a particularly long, loving letter but one paragraph disturbed him greatly. He was certain she had not meant to upset him, but she did mention going to a fall festival party at the First Presbyterian Church one night with John Paige, a local boy whose chronic asthma kept him out of the service.

A harmless, sociable evening no doubt, he thought. "Johnny Paige, however, wants to keep away from my preserves or he may get hurt," is what he wrote that night in his diary.

General Hooker's camp at the base of Lookout Mountain, Tennessee.

Chapter 11
Battle in the Clouds

> *November 24, 1863 ... "Shortly before daybreak we moved out of our reserved position and were busy setting up rude breastworks when the Rebs with very good range opened up on us with lively artillery fire. The crashing, shrieking and bursting of solid shot and shell through the woods as day was dawning will not be soon forgotten ... The storming and taking of Lookout by Hooker this afternoon was a brilliant affair, and with less loss than anyone supposed possible."*

Early that morning, the 11th Corps moved on the Confederate position at Cravens Farm along the western side of the slopes of Lookout Mountain. This was a diversional tactic, designed to enable Hooker and the 10th to move up Lookout and sweep the Rebs off that lofty base. The plan had been devised by a council of generals at the Chattanooga headquarters of Gen. U.S. Grant, who was in charge of operations. With him were William T. Sherman, Joseph Hooker and George H. Thomas.

The artillery had just gotten their guns in place and breastworks had been hastily thrown up when the Confederates in the lower part of the valley set up a barrage, soon to be followed by a rush of their infantrymen. Line after line of men in butternut poured rifle fire into the Union barricades. Charles and the men of the 119th were in the center of that onrush as the two brigades of the 11th Corps gave the Rebels a hot reception.

The 73rd Pennsylvania on the right, wavered and seemed about to break and run out, but they rallied and the near panic was stayed. The battle was waged in fierce intensity for more than an hour, and neither side could gain sufficient advantage to advance on the other. In mid-morning, there came a slackening of firepower from the Rebel position and the Union troops were ordered forward, from behind the breastworks and the thick growth of small trees at the base of the mountain.

Charles and Lloyd were fighting side by side through the whole battle sequence as Company C held its ground throughout.

"Let's go, let's go, men! We've got 'em on the run now, so let's finish it off!" Charles shouted jubilantly as they moved rapidly toward the Confederate position. There was only sporadic firing, however, and when the blue troops reached the embankment where the enemy had made its stand, they found the remnants of the Rebel brigade in full retreat along the ridge of the mountain.

Later that day, Charles and the others who were at Cravens Farm learned that they were the only ones engaged in actual battle that day — even though Hooker's troops scaled the palisades about noon and took the mountain fortress without opposition. They had been surprised that they moved upwards through the low misty clouds without much opposition from above, even more amazed to find the top deserted. There had been more climbing than fighting in the mists, an encounter which forever afterward would be known as "The Battle in the Clouds". Rather than risk being cut off from the main Confederate forces on Missionary Ridge, General Bragg had evacuated all of his troops from Lookout Mountain and the valley below. And now the U.S. flag flew atop Lookout Point.

* * * * * *

The next day, the men of the 119th joined the fighting to clear Missionary Ridge of Confederate strongholds. Charles and his company were with Hooker's command sweeping the first two hills successfully, as Sherman and Thomas moved forward on either side.

By mid-afternoon, the rifle pits were taken and the Rebels retreated to the high ridge. In their enthusiasm at having taken the lower positions, Union troops on all sides charged up the slopes and took the ridge. Bragg's center was broken and so were his right and left. Slowly he withdrew into Georgia with only rearguard action against Hooker's advancing troops . . . which included the 11th Corps.

As they passed Thomas' troops at Linor Station, both Union armies in pursuit of the enemy, Charles could not help but feel the exuberance of victory and see it etched on the faces of the men in blue passing by, their rifles held high in salute. During the day they met and took prisoner a number of Confederate stragglers. These men hadn't had a meal in several days and doubtless hadn't much sleep either. Charles spoke to one of them, a boyish-faced soldier busily gulping down corn mush at the time, and was told that Bragg's army was "pretty well used up."

On Sunday, November 29, the troops marched about 20 miles to Cleveland, Tenn. It must have been a pretty place before armies began using it as a crossroads, Charles thought as they entered the quaint village, filled with small but neat homes on narrow, tree-lined streets. Even the ravages of war had not entirely destroyed its attractiveness.

The corps bivouacked overnight in a large grove at the other end of town, but Charles and other officers got permission to sleep out of camp. It was arranged through Capt. Earl Southworth of the 119th, who had talked for some time with a local physician who invited him "and as many of you who can come" to spend the night at his home. So it was that Southworth, Hall, Lt. Marvin Moore, Charles and Lloyd called at Dr. Hunt's residence about 6 p.m. and were seated around a dining table less than a half hour later.

Hunt was a bachelor and hired a black woman as his housekeeper and cook. The house was a wood-sided, gabled cottage with a large porch that looked out upon the main street from the center of town. This was where the doctor and his guests sat after a sumptuous dinner of baked ham, spiced with tiny kernels of clove, along with candied yams, delicious blueberry scones, corn relish and tea.

"We don't have this every night, gentlemen, I can assure you," the genial doctor said as they were enjoying a brandy out on the porch. "As you must know, our troops are hard put for clothes and provisions, so we have no more livestock in the yard and the garden has been raided each time an army passes through. However, we do manage to squirrel away some of life's delicacies — such as that ham I smoked out back two years ago, and this brandy which is about the last I was able to buy last year in Memphis. I do, however, consider this an occasion to play host to my friends from up North."

Hunt, a general practitioner, was a strong Union man and he made no bones about it.

"Tennessee is filled with folks just like me, who feel we should never have seceded. We love the South and its people . . . we and our forebears have always lived here and expect to die here, but to sever all ties with the Union before settling the slavery issue is folly in its worst form. Think of the young men wasted, the anguish of families on both sides, when we as a young nation should be moving forward instead of fighting, brother against brother."

His family before him had followed a tradition of keeping bonded servants.

"Although they were always treated fairly, and with proper respect, they were still slaves," Hunt said. "That was something I could not condone when I was young, and when I moved here to go into practice, I bought Althea's contract and hired her to be my housekeeper. Whether she goes up North after this war is over or stays with me is to be her choice alone . . . but I rather believe she will stay."

Charles slept well that night, the first time in a "civilian bed" for some months, and breakfast the next morning was equally gratifying. The five Union officers cordially thanked Dr. Hunt for his hospitality and left to rejoin the regiment. It was Lloyd who summed it up.

"Know what, men? I've got a different feeling for this war, having spent the night with the good doctor and listening to his viewpoints. It seems as though we should all stop what we're doing and talk it over."

* * * * * *

It was a long, tedious march but the 11th, 14th and 15th corps were pushing toward Knoxville to relieve General Burnside, shut up and besieged by Longstreet's rebel troops.

The weather turned a damp chill which seemed to gnaw at the bones. Charles caught cold and it settled in the bowels. "This belly of mine is always raising the devil," he griped to Lloyd, "but if a Johnnie so much as catches me with my pants down, I'll pop him good!"

They broke camp early on December 12, crossed the Hiawassee and reached Athens by dusk. Charles was in charge that night in placing the picket line through an almost impenetrable woods, and it was most difficult to position the men so they could be readily relieved or be any use to themselves or others in case of attack. He left Lt. Jerry Mann in command when it was done.

About midnight, it was pitch dark and very cold when Charles made the grand rounds of the picket line and found the men suffering. They reported that they had been on post for three or four hours without relief. He thought the men imagined the time longer than it really was, owing to the cold and discomfort — until he reached picket headquarters. There he found Mann and every man of the reserve fast asleep. He roused them with a few choice words, sent them out on relief, and called Mann aside.

"Jerry, you no-good son-of-a-bitch . . . you've left the entire command exposed to the enemy with this neglect of our own men on the line! I'm mortified that such a thing should be done by an officer and men of the 119th. This is criminal conduct and I've a good mind to order you under arrest and send you back to headquarters!"

Mann, clearly shaken by his thoughtlessness, ran a hand nervously through his touseled hair as he begged Charles to let him off. He had never done this before, and knew there was no excuse even though he was fatigued, but if given a break this time he promised to more than make up for it. Charles was silent for a few moments, finally relented.

"All right, Jerry, even though I should never even listen to you, I will go against my better judgment and not say anything about this. But remember, damn you . . . one more slip and I throw the book at you!"

The early morning of December 2, the march to Knoxville was resumed and lasted all day until the troops stopped overnight at a small village called Philadelphia. "It's a pity they couldn't have gotten a bigger name," Charles mused. "There are more letters in the name than people in the place!"

They broke camp early the next day and marched a short ways to a town called London, on the banks of the Tennessee. It had been occupied by a small body of Rebels who fled on approach of the Federals, leaving behind a large quantity of stores and a hospital full of wounded Johnnies. These wounded, it was learned, had been gathered in from a number of small fights between Burnside and Longstreet in the neighborhood of Knoxville. From them, they learned that Bragg had stepped down as commander of the Army of the Tennessee but was retained by CSA President Jeff Davis as his military adviser . . . much to the chagrin of the fighting men.

In walking through the infirmary that afternoon, talking to some of the wounded, Charles met the rebel army surgeon who was left in charge of the hospital. There was something vaguely familiar about the man, who introduced himself as Dr. Lon Whitridge of South Carolina. He, in turn, looked quizzically at Charles, then spotted the Chi Psi pin on the latter's jacket.

A large man, he threw up both arms and lumbered forward like a kodiak bear on attack when Charles introduced himself.

"By gawd, your face looked familiar as hell the minute I saw you!" the other exclaimed as he pumped Charles' hand. "You do know me, don't you . . . I'm still your fraternity brother, Lon Whitridge, if you're the same Charley Lewis we used to call the damned little Greek root?"

It was two and a half years since Whitridge and some twenty other Union College undergrads left campus by early May 1861 to return to their homes in the South, presumably to enter military service. Charles remembered him well, a senior at the time, good-natured and bent on ribbing him in particular as a freshman member of the house. Now, though brothers fraternally, they were enemies in a struggle to the death.

Since he was free the rest of the day, Charles spent most of the time with Whitridge at the hospital and they enjoyed a pleasant reunion of sorts, drinking and talking together. The young officer was refreshed by the unexpected meeting, but deep in thought as he walked back to the encampment on the fringe of the town.

"He is as ardent a Rebel as I am Union, but we've got much in common to talk about . . . and he seemed mighty glad to meet someone from old Schenectady. I wonder, when this is all over and some of us are still alive, will there be a time when we can take up where we left off . . . or will the hurt take too long to heal?"

The next day they moved to within ten miles of Knoxville before bivouac late that evening. Unless Longstreet raised the siege, he would be sandwiched between Burnside and the reserve unit. Then word came that Longstreet had cleared out, so Burnside would need no assistance from the three corps that had been rushing to his aid. "Gad, I hope our march back will be less rapid than the forward one has been!" friend Lloyd spouted as they turned in.

However, they moved out early for a return movement to Chattanooga. While passing back through London, Charles saw Whitridge watching them from outside the hospital and ran over to grip his hand and say goodbye "till this cruel war is over."

The Capitol in Washington with its unfinished dome in 1863.

Chapter 12
A Visit With Seward

> *December 31, 1863 . . . "Mustered out for pay. The old year going out tonight in a fierce and blustery way has been an eventful one for me; and one in which I have gained I suppose much of what is called experience. Where will I be at the close of '64? Perhaps under the sod with Peissner. Tramped with Lloyd yesterday to the top of Lookout. The ascent is very steep and tiresome, but the view from the top is magnificent. It will always be a wonder how Hooker managed to get the Rebels so easily off this mountain. There must have been in their command a screw loose somewhere. Understand my leave, granted, is at corps headquarters; so it likely will reach me tomorrow — a New Year's gift."*

Charles picked up his 27-day furlough papers and left the camp in Lookout Valley the late afternoon of January 2. He and another officer, Capt. Charles Odell, took the trains and through wintry storms most of the way rode up through Nashville, Louisville, Cincinnati, Cleveland and Buffalo, staying at hotels overnight in several of the cities. At Buffalo, the morning of January 8, Odell took the Erie to New York City and Charles went on to Schenectady via the New York Central, arriving about 3 p.m. at the same dilapidated station which was a welcome sight.

The five months he had been away this time had seemed an eternity up until he was met at the door of the Lewis house by none other than his beloved Kate. She and the others had been waiting there for him since mid-morning, not knowing which train he might be on, and they saw him alight from the horse cab in front of South College.

Charles dropped his canvas bag and eagerly accepted her rush into his arms, embracing with a kiss that he had been dreaming of since last August. Finally, he held her out at arms-length, his eyes twinkling unabashed.

"Kate, Kate, my love . . . let me look at you! Can it be possible . . . that you have grown even more lovely?"

"No more than what you think you may see, Captain. Actually, I have grown older much faster since last summer, worrying about you, and I'm sure it must show," she said with a blush, slipping back into his arms. "But it is all your fault, you know, for staying away so long."

Now everyone had gathered around them — Father and Mother Lewis, Tayler, Maggie and the children — and took turns greeting the returning warrior. It dawned on him just then that the family had arranged this pleasant scenario, to remain apart until the two lovers had properly greeted each other.

Inwardly, he was relieved to see that Kate was given, and had accepted, the role as chairman of the reception committee.

School had been recessed over the holidays until the following week, but "I'd have stayed away, anyway, for today . . . regardless of whether they could get a substitute," Kate said.

After dinner, everyone gathered in the parlor and listened to Charles as he recounted his latest experiences.

"My arm's in fairly good shape, as good as it'll probably ever be, and I have managed to stay well otherwise, too. I must be carrying a lucky charm — and it may be my Chi Psi pin here," he laughed, having already told them about his chance meeting with Lon Whitridge. Most of his stories were on the lighter side, and told one about his train trip just completed.

"A snow storm accompanied us most of the way and delayed us a good deal. There was an accident between Nashville and Louisville in which the rear car broke its coupling as we were leaving a station, jumped the track and rolled down a hill steep enough to throw it entirely over. All the passengers were thrown into a heap but luckily only two or three were hurt, and they but slightly."

Another affair that might have been serious, but was only amusing, occurred in the middle of the night between Louisville and Cincinnati.

"The engine and all the cars, save ours, the rear one, in some way broke loose and left us stranded on the track by ourselves. The conductor luckily was with us, though someone else might have shown his foresight. We remained in this absurd position about an hour, or until we were missed at the next station, when the engineer ran the train back for us. In the meanwhile, the track being a single one, the conductor had gone back a ways and built a fire on the track as a warning to any coming train . . . and from this incident, a funny thing happened.

"There were seated near Odell and me a couple who had, as we learned from their conversation, been married the night before and were now on their wedding tour. The bride was evidently much older than the husband, but this in no wise repressed the ardor of their devotion. This love-making was most persistent, and constantly and utterly indifferent to the many smiles it caused around them.

"When the fire blazed up, someone cried out, 'Here comes an engine!' and, as no one had known of the conductor's lighting a fire in back of us, there was at once a lively rush from the car. The brave bridegroom made one leap from his seat and was out in the snow before one could say 'boo', leaving his old but very loving spouse to get out as best she could. Odell and I had the honor of escorting the frightened dame to safe quarters. One would have thought the husband's neglect might have cooled her ardor when the scare was over . . . but no! He was all she had or was likely to get, and they billed and cooed all the way to Cincinnati."

* * * * * *

The days went by all too quickly, but were well spent as far as Charles was concerned. He and Kate were together as much as her work schedule permitted, but there was also an important four-day trip which Charles and his father made to Washington two weeks after his return home.

Its object was to obtain a commission for Charles in the regular army, one which would lead to higher ranking and responsibilities. They went directly to the offices of Secretary of State William H. Seward on appointment, and were warmly welcomed upon being ushered in. The Auburn-born cabinet member was a good friend of Tayler Lewis because the two of them had been at Union together. Seward graduated in 1820 at age 19, while Lewis won his degree two years later at age 20. They embraced each other and vigorously shook hands.

"How are you, Ty, old chap! You're a sight for sore eyes and, by golly, just seeing you brings back some wonderful memories . . . and we thought *we* had some cares in those days!"

"That's right Bill, ours were the days when a student's main worry was passing end-of-semester exams. Now it's whether he should finish or fight," the professor responded, shaking his head sadly.

Charles was flattered to be greeted on a first name basis by such a notable figure as Secretary Seward, but amazed that he should know so much about his army record. The slight, white-haired executive had motioned for both visitors to be seated as he walked around his desk and sat down to examine a sheaf of papers before him. He leaned back in his swivel chair, turning toward Charles, and smiled encouragingly.

"As soon as I received your father's request, I contacted the war office and had them send over a copy of your service record to date. I must say, Charles, you've been a busy officer in recent times . . . wounded, the survivor of a major battle, and ever since in the midst of numerous forays against the enemy. I see no black marks against your record, only exemplary leadership within your state volunteer regiment . . . all of which makes me believe there is a good chance of getting a new appointment for you. Understand though, Captain Lewis . . . it might take some time to go through the necessary channels, but we will push it as strongly as we can."

They stayed only a short time, having already been alerted that the secretary was due at a cabinet session within the hour. However, the apologetic Seward insisted they come to dinner at his residence, near the White House, that evening at eight.

"Perhaps we can talk a bit more about your application, Charles," he said. "It will also give me a chance to relax a bit, I assure you. Just to renew some old times with your father could work wonders."

The Lewises, staying overnight at the posh Willard, kept the dinner date and did not return until nearly 11 p.m. The Sewards were gracious hosts, and Charles, for one, came away bubbling with enthusiasm over their visit.

"I must be honest, Father, but I always believed Mr. Seward accepted the cabinet post after Lincoln's election just to be first in line to see the president fall on his face. I thought he came down here sulking over losing the nomination to a rail-splitter . . . but after what we heard tonight, I know I was wrong."

Tayler Lewis nodded in agreement.

"I, too, may have shared those same thoughts months ago . . . and I cannot say as I would blame him under the circumstances, because Bill Seward may never again get the chance he had in '60. He would have made a good president, I'm sure, but now he is proving himself a worthy statesman. Naturally, as an old Union man, I'm proud of him."

"And Charles, if anyone can get you that promotion, he can," the professor added as an afterthought.

* * * * * *

Back at the hotel, before retiring, the two were still discussing their after-dinner conversations with the Sewards and one was particularly poignant to both. It had to do with a young man by the name of James G. Johnson, yet a student at Union College.

The secretary mentioned him first, asking Tayler Lewis whether he knew how Johnson was taking to college life.

"Jimmy came down here in the late Fifties and served for a time in my office when I was senator," Seward said. "I liked the boy tremendously. He was an excellent bookkeeper and file clerk, and showed great promise of becoming someone better than office help. What I did was to promise him a job in my law office if he'd go on to college and get a degree. Of course, I recommended our old alma mater and away he went . . . up to Schenectady and greater things. He wrote soon after he got there, but I haven't heard from him since."

It was then that both Charles and his father told him about the accident in which Johnson lost the lower part of his right leg.*

"He was doing well in classes I thought, and fit in well with the boys at Kappa Alpha," Professor Lewis began. "It must have been the end of '61 when it happened. He was in downtown Schenectady, rather late and it was dark and snowy, when he tried to get past a stalled freight train at the Union Street crossing. He was jumping over the coupling between cars when his foot slipped on the ice and he fell beneath the car just as the train began moving. He tried to crawl out past the wheels, but they passed over one of his legs, just above the ankle."

Charles told how the campus rallied behind the unfortunate student, raising money to help pay hospital expenses at Albany, where he had been taken after the accident.

*See "The Johnsons of Union College" page 139.

"He was a real good man, and we were glad when he came back the next spring . . . on crutches but in good spirits. As far as I know, he's still there but should graduate next year . . . the same as I would be, under different circumstances."

The professor looked with a grin at Seward as he said: "I must tell you some sad news however, Bill. Your boy will not be coming back to you as a lawyer, after all. Johnson has the bearing and inclination of a clergyman. I sensed it less than a week after he was in my theology class, and discussed the possibility of his following the Lord and his teachings toward the goal of becoming a preacher. It was after the accident he told me that he had decided to do just that. I am sure he will make a fine minister."

"My dear friend, please do not apologize for removing a budding lawyer from our society," Seward laughed as he hunched forward in mock earnestness. "From what I hear, there are too many of us as it is . . . while on the other hand, mankind is seriously in need of spiritual uplifting. Here's to pastor Johnson . . . may he reign supreme in his life's work."

Chapter 13
Promise of Spring

February 12, 1864 . . . "The hours and days with Kate have of course been delightful and I dread the thought of bidding her goodbye tonight. She and Maggie and brother Tayler will see me off on the train, and then I will plunge into the darkness alone and leave them and all the joys of old Schenectady behind me. Their hearts, and especially Kate's, will I know be sad and heavy, and I shall have all I can do to keep back the salt drops, but perhaps a kind fate will bring all of us together again."

That day he had taken Kate out to her school in the morning and returned with her in the afternoon, a routine they had followed most of the weekdays Charles was at home. They were all to have dinner in the Lewis house at eight, but the returning soldier spent some time alone up in his room earlier in the evening. He enjoyed a last warm bath and shave at the household, put on a freshly laundered and ironed uniform, sat down at the front window overlooking the pasture and city below.

It was a bleak winter's day. Snow lay in patches among dried brown grass and through the bare tree limbs along Union Street he could see the chimney smoke rising from the houses down that way. In the fast-dying twilight, it made a particularly striking, homey picture, Charles thought. He was to leave from the station at midnight, and now he was gathering his thoughts and courage about an always dubious future, pausing every so often as he wrote in his diary.

"The longed-for vacation is about over, and soon its joys and the sweetness of its pleasures will be but a memory; but the recollection of these thirty-two days will not soon fade, while thoughts and memories of many pleasant incidents crowded into them will cheer many a lonely hour in camp and on the picket line . . . Katie, darling, you have been wonderfully sweet during these happy, happy days and when I forget thee, may my right hand forget its cunning . . . May God bless and keep all, and bring us all together if it be His will, when the struggle and the fight is over; but in any event, may the strength be given us to do our whole duty, and every part of it."

* * * * * *

He was back in camp at Shellmound, Tenn., early the morning of February 20, and found that Lloyd already had their winter quarters fixed up with ingenious "comforts of home."

The welcome was cordial and Charles found it pleasant to see the tanned, smiling faces of Lloyd, Willis, Hall, Moore, Southworth and the fellows of the company. For the moment, at least, the regrets that had been with him since leaving the Schenectady station were forgotten.

The Army of the Cumberland was preparing for permanent occupation of that area. The Confederates had been driven entirely from the Tennessee hills and now Bragg's beaten army lay in winter quarters at Dalton, Ga., holding the railroad to Atlanta.

The officers and men of the 119th New York were all housed in log huts, using army tents for the roofs. Lloyd had constructed a stone fireplace during his sidekick's absence, and had made a number of chairs, shelves, a writing table — even a rocking chair — out of ammo boxes and scrap lumber. The energetic lieutenant also had inveigled a staff orderly to get a couple of framed pictures, both of them tinted engravings of Mississippi riverboats, to hang on the walls.

"Mighty cozy . . . quite a shebang* you've made here!" Charles said approvingly as he first stepped into their quarters. "Why, I'd marry you in a minute, Lieutenant, if you weren't already spoken for!"

One of the projects backfired, however. The day before Charles arrived, Lloyd had pasted up water-proofed paper on the inside of the log walls, ostensibly to keep out drafts. He used flour paste and it attracted hordes of field mice. The rustling of their midnight snacks made sleep in the hut impossible so, next day, all the paper was ripped off.

The weather had turned pleasant. The roads were dry, the result of several weeks of warm southerly breezes, so Lloyd and Charles mounted up and galloped over the terrain on several of the days they were off duty. They were riding one day out of Chattanooga, along a dusty hardpan, and pulled to a stop, admiring for a few minutes the beauty of the country around them. It was a sunny morning, and bare fields rolled away from the hills and mountains which blazed with colors that, at home, would be called autumnal wonder. Birds of every description fluttered about, feeding from field plants, chirping from tree branches.

"Gawd, what a place . . . what beautiful country!" Lloyd enthused. "It's hard to believe, with all this, that we're here and the enemy is just a ways over the mountains there, both of us biding time before we're at one another's throats again. Long after all of us are gone, long after this war is over, those timeless hills out there will be looking down on new generations of Americans, maybe tilling these fields, building new homes. Is there any assurance that those people will know that few of us enjoy spilling the other's blood . . . that we're enemies not out of hatred but for a cause which maybe only the Almighty God will decide must prevail?"

*See "Civil War Potpourri" page 137.

"I really don't know, my friend. I've thought along those lines myself, plenty of times since putting on this uniform, but all I know is that we can't go soft until the last shot is fired . . . and as long as you have waxed philosophical, let me say that if we're interested in staying alive we must make damned sure Johnny Reb knows we won't shake hands until he drops his gun."

* * * * * *

Soon after his return, Charles visited the quarters of the 134th New York in Lookout Valley and found that Lt. Col. Clinton C. Brown was in acting command. Allen Jackson had a finger blown off the previous month and had gone back to Schenectady on leave. Brown, also a Schenectadian, entertained Charles all that afternoon, anxious to hear firsthand all the hometown news his guest could tell him.

In mid-March, Charles and Lloyd presented themselves before the army board of examiners and applied for the positions of colonel and lieutenant colonel, respectively. After a written and oral examination, they were told by a Colonel Lurn, presiding officer, that they would be notified in the field or as soon as possible.

If successful, and both felt confident, they would be transferred to the regular army as officers of the colored troops then being organized in Pennsylvania. It was something the two friends had talked over for some time, finally deciding to make the move. As they left the unit office, Charles draped an arm over the shoulder of Johnny Lloyd, then clapped him on the back.

"By God, old man, I think we did it . . . I **know** we did it! We're ripe for the job and our credentials passed without a hitch. Did you see them nod to each other after the exams? Lloyd, just think . . . I'll bet in another month you and I will be commanding new outfits up North, but we'll have some leave time before we march again. We've done ourselves proud this day!"

Strangely, Lloyd was solemn.

"I guess so, but suddenly — now that the opportunity is within our grasp — I wonder, do I really do have the capacity to command? It's a terrible responsibility . . . all those men, putting their trust in someone who's been soldiering only a year and a half."

"Stow it, Lloyd. You're a good officer, I know that for a fact. I'd never have let us make application if I didn't firmly believe we're both going to do a helluva job. So what say we do a little celebrating tonight . . . to the two Colonels of the Nawth!"

Chapter 14
Death at Resaca

April 18, 1864 . . . "The 11th and 12th Corps have been consolidated, to be called the 20th, under command of General Hooker. Our regiment with the 134th NY, 33rd NJ, and 27th Pa compose the 2nd Brigade, 2nd Division. Active operations will begin soon in all probability. The weather is just becoming settled; the roads are in good condition, and in a few days the large force gathered hereabouts will be in motion under the great general, William Tecumseh Sherman."

As the soft springtide at last brought blossoms to trees and a brighter green to the river banks, a note of preparation was sounding in the camps of the Army of the Cumberland at Chattanooga and Lookout Valley. General Grant was no longer with them. On March 10 he had been named general of all the Union armies, while Halleck was relegated to a desk job as Chief of Staff. Meanwhile, Hooker, McPherson and Thomas remained in Tennessee, under supreme command of Sherman.

During their winter sojourn at Lookout, the mass of Federal troops had spent several months of drilling, picket watches, card playing and camp rumoring, not necessarily in that order. It was a time when soldiering became a bore, when cleaning a rifle every day became an hour's ritual just to occupy the mind. The men were thinking of home and how much they could be doing on the home front rather than lolling about camp, hundreds of miles from their home town.

Lloyd started a garden back of the log hut and now had several rows of yellow beans and black-eyed peas nearly at the "pickin' stage". Other men took up hobbies of wood carving, making small images of Reb soldiers, Tennessee mountaineers, and river boats. There was even a soldier in the 134th New York who received an artist's set in a package from home, and for weeks had taken to producing water colors of local scenery which he sold to the highest bidders.

All this began to change by mid-April when word came that the two corps, the 11th and 12th, had become the 20th . . . and that moving out day was fast approaching. Soon after May 3, the huge army began its march through Georgia. Object: Annihilation of Confederate generals Joseph E. Johnston's and John Bell Hood's armies of the Tennessee and the capture of Atlanta.

Sherman's task would not be an easy one and he knew it, but he started out with confidence that he could whip his formidable opponents, Johnston in particular. Sherman's men had confidence in him, too. Whenever they saw "Uncle Billy and his white socks", the Union men in blue were ready to roll.

However, those 135 miles between Chattanooga and Atlanta in the end would require three grueling, hard-fought months to cover.

Except for a few brief skirmishes with the retreating enemy, the 20th Corps pressed its march through Peavine, Ringgold, Whiteport Church, Buzzard Roost Gap, and Dogwood Valley along hot, dusty roads that swirled choking alkali into the throats of the marchers, through low swampy regions infested with snakes and mosquitoes. Occasionally there was a halt in the column as the officer in charge of the pioneer corps noticed a bad spot in the road which must be corduroyed before the wagons could pass. Hundreds of detailed men quickly tore down fence rails, hacked down pine saplings and threw them into the gully. Then the march resumed.

Early in the evening, camp sites were selected — usually in the vicinity of water and on high slopes — and in no time at all, the men had their shelter tents up and sputtering fence rails burning in front of them. The wagons parked and the animals fed, the men then took care of their own rations. Campfires danced and flared upward until the call "Out lights! Out lights!" Then the three o'clock fires burned dimly and everything was silent except for the occasional neighing of the horses.

* * * * * *

The march to Atlanta in those first two weeks was no picnic but easier than expected. Suddenly, Hood's division made a stubborn stand at Resaca.

On the morning of May 15, as the 20th Corps moved towards Resaca, the 1st Division was soon engaged as enemy cannonading resounded throughout the countryside. The 2nd Division was held in reserve until early afternoon, and it was then that the 119th New York moved out with its division to join the ongoing battle.

Charles was leading Company C and Lloyd was just behind with Company F as the regiment was quickly deployed, and with the rest of the brigade charged into a wood thick with underbrush. Once through, the troops ran across an open field toward a hill, the summit of which was a lunette with four big guns. The rifle fire of the Rebels was very sharp, and the cannon in the lunette gave the charging Federals heavy doses of grape and canister.

As he rallied his men in the race up the hill, Charles could not make out the Confederate line of battle, only the bright flashes of rifle and cannon fire from the hilltop. This sector must be strictly artillery, he figured, and if they could make it in the next five minutes, they'd take the hill with minimal loss of life.

"Come on, come on! Move on 'em, men . . . Let's take the hill and we're home free!" he screamed above the din.

They did just that. The line surged forward, never stopping until it reached the Rebel breastworks, and the infantry went over in a riot of jubilation as the Confederates threw down their rifles and surrendered. The lunette, its guns, and many prisoners were taken in this phase of the Battle of Resaca, and at a relatively low casualty rate.

However, to Charles, they paid dearly for the victory . . . and the costliest price was the gallant Lloyd.

The two were close together on the hill, urging the men forward, and were near the summit when a bullet struck Lloyd just above the hip, passed clean through and in its course severed the main artery. As the stricken man staggered back, Charles saw the ashen hue of death spread over his features and feared the worst for his best friend. He at once ordered two men to pick up the fallen officer and carry him down the hill out of range of fire.

Once the company was relieved, a despondent Captain Lewis hurried over to the field hospital to see if Johnny Lloyd still lived. A physician in attendance checked his list of dead and wounded, looked up at Charles and shook his head slowly, side to side.

"I'm sorry, Captain, but he was barely alive when he was brought here. There was nothing we could do to stop the bleeding, and he had lost too much already."

Charles asked to see the body, to say goodbye to Lloyd, who never spoke after the slug struck him. As he lifted the blanket and looked down upon his friend's dead face, a strong kindly face now so calm and peaceful, he thought of the pleasant times they had together, his many kindnesses, his cheery voice. And Charles could not restrain the tears.

That night, the troops bivouacked on the other side of Resaca and would move out in the morning, perhaps to re-engage the enemy just the other side of the hills to the southeast. Charles was dog-tired, as were most of the men who were in the battle lines, and they rolled into their blankets early after mess. Tomorrow would be another day, but before he sank into deep sleep, the sorrowing young officer thought of Lloyd's poor wife.

"This is Sunday night, and she is up there in New York City probably thinking of the man who loved her truly but now lies here, cold and dead . . . I must write to her very soon . . . but it won't be easy."

Chapter 15
On Atlanta's Doorstep

> *May 17, 1864... "Sent forward an application to be mustered out of the 119th and into the 178th. I greatly miss Lloyd; for me at least the whole life of the regiment seems to have been taken."*

Monday morning the troops were ready for marching before dawn. Hooker was in a hurry to get after the retreating Confederates and the 20th was on the move as light broke over the misty landscape. There was, however, no opposition to be encountered the other side of the Resaca hillside. The enemy, as Charles later noted in his diary, had "folded their tents and silently stolen away."

The Union army marched on all that day, finally encamping after crossing the Ostenaula River. Mail was distributed that evening, the postal wagon having caught up to the corps headquarters. Charles was seated alone in his tent when an orderly gave him a packet of letters, and he settled back to read some news from home. Just what he needed to cure a gloomy mood.

Ironically, the mail did just the opposite. Notice had reached both Charles and Lloyd that they had successfully passed the examination for command of colored troops, as colonel and lieutenant colonel, respectively. There also was official notification from the war office in Washington City that Charles had been awarded a major's commission in the 178th New York.

He was stunned, and lay back on his cot to think matters over. Seward's connection had come through with the new commission and appointment to regular army . . . and that would be the course of action, Charles decided.

"Now that Lloyd is gone, I'll decline the first appointment," he mused. "I never had any great love for the service, and only applied to serve with him. So now I'm a major, a big shot major, and soon will be with a new outfit . . . but it means little to me. Lloyd's death makes the ties binding me to the 119th still lighter."

Later that night, Charles wrote a long letter to Kate telling her the grim news about friend Lloyd, and of his decision to accept the major's commission in a new regiment. There was, however, a preponderance of words of love and longing which grew into four pages of what the men commonly referred to as "hometown mush". The lonesome soldier wound up with a flourish.

"Oh, what I wouldn't give for even a brief glimpse of you, darling Katie . . . and a long sweet kiss on your dear lips. This is, however, a devil of a time and place for kissing. I cannot have it and there is no use in growling or mooning over it. My dear girl, you long for me no more than I long for you."

* * * * * *

The Union armies encountered some spotty but brisk fighting in various sectors as the march to Atlanta wore on. Just outside Calhoun, on Howard's right, there was some hard fighting for several hours and the 3rd Division of the 10th had to bear part of the battle against Hood's men. Later that day, the whole corps moved forward once more and set up camp within a few miles of Kingston.

It was here that the corps rested a few days while advance units sought out the best routes through central Georgia and an inkling where the strongest units of the Confederates were located along that line of march. Charles was in command of the skirmish line the next day. They saw no Rebels, but got very tired from the irregular tramping over the hills, through fields, and amongst briars and underbrush.

On the second day of bivouac at Kingston, Charles joined several of the men for a swim in a mill pond nearby. Diving into the cold, greenish water put him in mind of the days in Schenectady when the college students frequented Wendell's quarry pond just above the campus. Aside from a nasty cut on his leg, caused by a brush against a nail in a sunken log, he spent an enjoyable afternoon. He was thoroughly pleased that his bad arm withstood the diving and stroking.

Soon after, however, Major Lewis would begin to have his problems.

On May 23rd, the army had moved out and crossed the Etowah River. In early afternoon the long lines stretched along a very dusty road, and the men were sweltering in the humidity and scorching sunlight. There were temporary halts, wherever some shade was handy, and the men just dropped in their tracks to rest a few minutes and sip water from their canteens. Their knives and canteens were stashed in their haversacks, by official order, to cut down on rattling noises during the march. With the enemy close at hand, it was better to avoid extraneous clatter warning him of an advance.

Charles was walking to the side of one of the columns when suddenly he collapsed and was placed in the horsedrawn ambulance. His head was splitting and soon he was shaking with fever and sickness. The company physician, Dr. George Gunkle, diagnosed his illness as sunstroke, but said he'd probably get over it if he kept out of the direct sunlight for several days.

Charles practically lived in the ambulance by day, following after the regiment on the long marches, then feeling sick and miserable during the night bivouacs. On May 25, the whole corps was involved at Dallas where both Hood and Johnston pushed their forces against the Yankees who were closing in on Atlanta. Inside the canvas-covered ambulance, Charles heard the roar and cracking of cannon and rifle and he fretted and fumed at his inactivity. Casualties were at a minimum, however, no one killed and less than a hundred wounded.

Hours after the fray, Dr. Gunkle looked in on Charles and said he was ordering him back to Nashville for hospitalization.

"We've got several wagons heading back with the more badly wounded,

Major, and I think it best you go with them. Your trouble could prove very serious unless you get perfect rest and quiet . . . and are wholly free from the heat and excitement of the march. Three weeks at Nashville may do wonders for you . . . we'll see."

After a long and tedious trip, one full of delays and annoyances, Charles was quartered in Room 48 at Officers Hospital in Nashville. With him were a Captain Fulsom of the 143rd New York and a Lieutenant Adams of General Ewing's staff. Just down the hall was Lt. Bob Moore of the 119th, being treated for a wounded lip and jaw. These were among the casualties of the Dallas fight.

His three-week "rest cure" did wonders. At least his head did not ache and throb when he went outdoors. His doctors cautioned him, however, against too much exposure to the sun for at least another month.

So back Charles went, rejoining his regiment encamped at Big Shanty, Ga., on June 24. They had been through thickly-pitched battles on the 15th and 16th, and were slowed but never fell back. There were some new men in the outfit, replacing some who were lost to battle.

In the days to come, the lines were so close that shot and shell were exchanged, sometimes so frequently it seemed like a constant battle until both sides settled down for evening chow and bed roll. The second day back, Charles took a turn as brigade officer and spent much of the time in the rifle pits with the men. Firing along much of the line was brisk and sharp and shells passed over them into camp. The lines were so close that relieving the pickets had to be done after dark. On that day, Capt. Jonathan Wheeler of the 13th Ohio battery was killed when cannon shot struck his tent. The day's loss to the 20th: three killed and twelve wounded.

Little by little, the Federals managed to push forward, a half mile at a time, as the Rebel advance skirmish lines gave way stingily. On July 3, Johnston vacated his outer line and the 20th Corps instantly moved in to occupy it. The ground troops were given rest as heavy artillery was moved up and supply wagons brought to the fore, ready for the big push on the last leg to Atlanta. Sherman sent out word to all the corps commanders that this was to be the all-out effort to reach the Georgia capital.

Just before it began, however, Charles was faced with a dilemma. His head had been pounding mercilessly again and near-fainting spells came frequently in the heat of the day. Col. Pat Jones, brigade commander, spotted the junior officer's problem upon returning from picket duty and sent him over to brigade headquarters. There Charles talked at length with the division surgeon-in-chief, a Colonel McCabe, who said there was only one solution — for Charles to quit the army.

"It will do no good to send you back to the hospital because you are all through fighting, Major. You are suffering from a severe case of sunstroke and it will not go away, but will get steadily worse, the longer you are down here. When I endorse this certificate on the state of your health, the only thing left is for you to forward your resignation."

So it was done and, pending final notice from headquarters, Charles Lewis would be a civilian once more. Meanwhile, there was fighting just ahead for Sherman's army and while he was still head of Company C, 114th Regiment, the sunstruck major was on active duty.

On July 20, at Peach Tree Creek, the last defenses of Atlanta, the Rebel army attacked in a desperate attempt to thwart the Yankee drive. The day before, President Davis had replaced "Retreating Joe" Johnston with the rash General Hood, and the latter lost no time in taking the initiative.

About noon, the 14th and 20th Corps were hit by Rebel infantry and artillery before there was barely time to throw up breastwork. The Federals were flanked badly on the left and for a time were exposed not only to direct fire but to a galling enfalading fire that threatened to break their lines. Just in the nick of time, however, the 1st and 3rd divisions joined the action and the day was saved. The dogged Johnny Rebs charged three times until about 5 p.m. but were repulsed each time with great slaughter. Hood's army fell back in the late afternoon.

Many were lost in the 20th, but Charles and the 114th fared better than most regiments. As for himself, he was amazed how little he was aware of his affliction until the last shot had been fired. Only then, he felt his head was bursting and the battlefield wavering before him. There were blackened stumps out there, strewn with the corpses of men in gray.

It was a costly battle for both sides, but especially for the South. The Union army had over 20,000 men involved, of which 1,600 were killed and wounded. Out of the nearly 19,000 men which the Confederates put in the field, there were about 2,500 killed or wounded.

Now Sherman's army ringed Atlanta north and east. On July 22, Hood attacked McPherson's Army of the Tennessee in the Battle of Atlanta itself, only to fail again. But brilliant James Birdseye McPherson was killed, replaced by Gen. O.O. Howard. This miffed Gen. Joe Hooker, who resigned.

"I don't blame him one bit," Charles growled. "He deserved the place, and is worth a dozen Howards."

On July 28, the Schenectady soldier was given official notice that his resignation had been received and accepted. Further, that a wagon train was leaving the next day for Marietta and the trip back home. Actually, he was now a civilian. That night he wrote in his diary:

"This is my last day in camp. It is mighty hard to say goodbye to the fellows, but I suppose it cannot be helped. I feel poorly and sick, but still am sorry I resigned. If I had the chance to do it over again, it would not be done. The desire to see home and loved ones is completely lost in regret at leaving here."

He was on the doorstep of Atlanta, but would not cross the threshold.

Chapter 16
A Citizen Comes Home

> *August 17, 1864 . . . "Have been feeling very poorly since my return, but think there is some improvement. Am unable, however, to stand to any extent the direct rays of the sun. Started this morning for Fort Miller; dined at the Thompson's and then crossed the river to Uncle Tayler's."*

Nearly two weeks passed before "Mister" Lewis arrived home from the morning he left Marietta, Ga., on July 29. He spent almost a week in Nashville getting his discharge papers and pay. After payment of all debts, he had $108 left, enough to make him feel tolerably wealthy. He also waited for the arrival of Lloyd's baggage, which he sent on to the sorrowing widow in New York City.

Charles rode the mail boat from Louisville to Cincinnati, a quiet scenic trip up the Ohio River, and then entrained from there through Cleveland and Buffalo to home. It was early morning when he reached the Schenectady station on Wednesday, August 10, and went up to the campus by horse cab. There was considerable luggage this time, all his worldly belongings as a veteran soldier of two years in the field.

Mother and Father Lewis had just finished breakfast as he walked in, not suspecting that he would be there until late afternoon. Charles had written two days earlier, indicating that he might be delayed until then. It made no difference. He was home, and was greeted with unabashed hugs, tears and laughter as when he first arrived on furlough.

Jane Keziah was beside herself. As she fixed breakfast for Charles, she kept wiping her eyes with the apron while looking at her son, seated at the kitchen table, as though he might vanish from sight. Professor Lewis was smiling broadly, saying little and nodding his head as Charles brought them up to date on his return trip. Their son was home, and home to stay.

Brother Tayler already had gone to his summer job as a cashier's clerk at the Schenectady Bank on lower State near Church Street. Not yet 17, the lad had just finished a year at Union and had visions of someday becoming a full-fledged banker. Maggie and her children were up at Fort Miller for the summer, and Kate . . . she was well, Mother Lewis said, and had planned on going down to the station with them in the afternoon.

Charles was anxious to see her, but after breakfast he bathed and shaved off traveling grime. He removed the uniform, he supposed, for the last time and barely managed to draw on the light herringbone trousers he last wore before going into service over two years ago. It was a warm day, so he wore only an

89

open-necked shirt without the attached collar and it was a bit tight around the shoulders. He rolled up the sleeves and the scar on his left arm was partly visible. At least his fancy square-toed, three-button lace shoes fit as before. He felt a bit sheepish as he came downstairs.

"Well, Mother, as you can see . . . your boy has grown in the army. One of the first things I must do is get some new clothes that fit. Tayler can have mine, unless he's into latest fads. But the really first thing I want to do now is get down to Franklin Street and see if my sweetheart still loves me!"

She did. Charles was given the hero's welcome in spades as they kissed, hugged and talked the rest of the morning away. Kate even made some lunch as the noon hour slipped by. They were alone. Brother Edward, back home after medical discharge, was at the broom factory. Mrs. Smith had died two months before.

"Charles, Charles, this has got to be the happiest day of my life . . . so far" Kate bubbled as she put their light repast on the kitchen table. "Just to think you will not ever be leaving again just makes me want to dance and shout hallelujah till the cows come home!"

He caught her by the waist as she began to spin on her tiptoes, arms upraised and skirt swirling about her, and kissed her passionately about the lips, neck and shoulders.

"You're no happier than I, my darling . . . and now perhaps we can begin thinking about our future together."

* * * * * *

Recurring headaches continued to plague Charles and it was recommended that he see Dr. Harman Pease, a specialist in such disorders. The doctor had converted the front room of his residence at 105 State St. into his practicing office and examining room. Just across the street, Charles could see the copper Indian and canoe ornament above the brownstone facade of the Mohawk Bank. It was a new building, the bank having moved into it seven years before from the old bank at Union and North Church. The sun's rays reflected in the plate glass windows, so he turned slightly to one side as Doctor Pease continued his diagnosis.

"I advise you to get complete rest, Mr. Lewis, and stay out of the bright sunlight. You have suffered from severe sunstroke and it is possible that you will continue to feel its effects for many weeks, maybe months. But take these precautions and there is every reason to think you will be a well man again before this year is out."

This was the day after his return from a three-day trip north. He had enjoyed the ride alone, passing through colorful Saratoga Spa and the hilly green countryside, spurring his roan at a fast pace across the bridge near Schuylerville, then slowing to a leisurely pace until he reached Fort Miller. This was where relatives of both the Peissners and Lewises lived, and Charles managed to visit them all — Uncle Tayler, Teet Lewis, Cousin Maggie, Clayton and Sam Thompson. Sister Maggie and children were staying at Uncle Tayler's for the summer.

No permanent gravestone had been placed yet at the grave of Elias Peissner in the cemetery beside Fort Miller Dutch Reformed Church, but there was a white wooden cross on which was inscribed: "Col. Elias Peissner, Commander of the 119th NY Volunteer Infty. Died a hero in the Battle of Chancellorsville, May 2, 1863."

Before recrossing the river to Gansevoort to stay for the night at the Thompson's, Charles picked some brilliant fireweed and placed them next to the marker. He knelt briefly as he offered a silent prayer, then stood for quite some time beside the grave as he thought of Elias and their last days together.

* * * * * *

November 8, 1864 . . . "Election Day. God grant the triumph of Union, Lincoln and the right."

So the summer crept slowly past. And as autumn came, tinted leaves from the maples which lined Union Street and from the elms on College Terrace lay thick in the front yards of the lower houses and up on College Hill. The trees tossed their bare limbs against the sky.

Charles was beginning to feel better. The headaches were infrequent and less severe. He had begun the study of law in the office of Johnson & Hill, located in the county annex at 15 Union St. It was at Father Lewis' urging that he took the job as file and research clerk, but he was not good at it.

The approaching national elections had everyone in Schenectady stirred to a fever pitch, Charles included. He could not cast a vote, since he would not be 21 until next June 14, but this was no deterrent when it came to expressing his views. He was strictly pro-Lincoln and there were many who came into the office touting the Democratic candidacy of Gen. George B. McClellan. Not strange. Schenectady County, largely Democratic, didn't support Lincoln in 1860 and was about to do the same in 1864.*

It galled Charles to hear some of the lawyers, judges and city dignitaries run down the president during some of the heated discussions over the election. Too many of them, he thought, blamed Lincoln for the long war, early reverses — even failure to "make an honorable peace." He sat at his desk, shuffling legal papers while gritting his teeth.

One day he could stand it no longer, and Judge Stephen A. Johnson, a county judge and surrogate, was disturbed when Charles spoke out against a tirade directed at Abraham Lincoln. He told his file clerk later that he viewed

---

**See "Civil War Potpourri" page 137.*

the outburst as "presumptuous on the part of a young man in my law firm who has yet to cut his baby teeth on the fundamentals of law and politics."

Johnson himself was a Lincoln man, and said he shared most of Charles' views on the election.

"However, my boy, you have a lot to learn about diplomacy and decorum," was his parting shot as he left the office that late afternoon.

The next day, Charles tendered his resignation as law apprentice. As he told his father: "I still feel I was within my rights to speak up against something I know to be wrong. I may not be 21, but I am a citizen and know something about this war. Another thing . . . Doctor Nott can call me 'my boy', but I don't fancy it coming from a pompous politician!"

The night of November 9, he wrote in his diary: "Was up all night checking returns down at the Daily Star. They put the announcements on an outside board as soon as they came in. As far as we can judge at this time, Lincoln has carried every state save Kentucky and New Jersey. No one now can doubt the successful termination of the war, in an honorable and patriotic way. The little ballots that dropped all over our land yesterday have settled the question of secession in this country."

The Erie Canal bridge over Liberty Street, looking west. Part of John Ellis' house can be seen at right center. Isaac Bancker's blacksmith shop is at left, other side of bridge. Hitching posts, gas lights and cobblestone paving are much in evidence.

Chapter 17
Love Grows Sour

> *Monday, November 28, 1864: "I must soon make up my mind as to which direction to take, leading ultimately to my life's work. I have an uneasy feeling that I am not destined for civilian employ, having survived the rigors of military service. But where does Kate fit into all this? I would not want ever to give her up."*

The happy homecoming and jubilation over his return to civilian life began to wear thin by mid-November, as far as Charles was concerned. Having quit his job at the law office, he was seriously considering reapplying for commission as head of a colored regiment but hadn't told anyone. He felt good health had returned, at least sufficient to pass a physical. Meanwhile, Father Lewis was urging him to begin the next semester at Union toward completing his studies.

"In a year and a half, you will have your degree and a good job will be open to you," the professor said. "My son, this is your only option if you sincerely wish to be a success."

All too simple, Charles thought. Just now, with the war on, he didn't feel like returning to the classroom. As a matter of fact, he was getting restless, bored with civilian life, and he was well aware that Kate knew it. In their last few times together, conversation grew stilted and their love-making amounted to a good-night kiss.

The crisis deepened one night as they returned to her house after a social at St. George's Church. Kate seemed preoccupied during the walk home, sometimes to the point of not hearing what he said. As they began crossing the canal bridge at Liberty Street, toward Isaac Bancker's weathered smithy, Charles suddenly stopped and took Kate gently by the arm.

"Katie, something's wrong between us. We both know it, but nothing's been said and it's time we talked. I haven't been good company lately, not even for myself, but right now my life is a little mixed up and I want you to know it isn't you. I love you so much, and losing you would be the end for me."

"Charles, you know I love you and I'll always love you, no matter what the future holds, but I must know something about us. Are we to be married soon, within the next year at least?"

"My darling, I worship you and want you for my wife," he said, drawing back in surprise, "but I must also know that I am able to support a wife and, I hope, a family. There is no other but you, Kate. . .that is why I must be worthy of you."

Charles reached out to draw her to him, but she pulled away.

"Please, Charles, hear me out, then do what you think best. I know what you must be going through, wondering where you fit into civilian life and all, but I must make plans for my own life. Either you're in them or you're not. I am not going to be a schoolmarm forever. Neither will I be a spinster. No, Charles, what my future holds for me is a husband and children, and I'd rather it be with you. I don't ask for wealth, only a happy home. . .and we could have that, I know. I ask only to be included in your plans for the new year. . .as your wife. It's all up to you."

"Kate, Kate. . .all I can say now is that I want you deeply, to share the rest of my life with you. Marry you? I'd do it tomorrow, with every fibre in my body throbbing with ecstacy. . .but please, Kate, give me more time to get things straightened out with my life, to know where I'm going and even what I will be doing to earn a living. I don't want to lose you sweetheart. Believe me, that's all that matters to me. I just want to be sure that I deserve you."

For a few minutes, both leaned on the bridge railing, looking north toward the Union Street crossing. The dark, shimmering canal was devoid of traffic as far as they could see. This was the last week before the sluice gates would be opened and the canal closed for the winter, and most boats had made their destinations by now. Finally, Charles put an arm about Kate's shoulders, pulled her to him and kissed her passionately.

As the two lovers walked back to Franklin Street, arm in arm, they said little. At the door, Kate turned to Charles and clasped him tightly with her arms.

"Oh, my darling, what shall I do with you? What's to be done about us?" She sobbed against his shoulder. "Let's say goodnight now and do some serious thinking about us. There has got to be a way we can make it work. . .and spend our life together."

Then Kate reached up and kissed him before she hurriedly went into the house. Charles was in a stupor as he walked up to South College. He felt everything was closing in on him, yet was glad that he and Kate had come to terms. He could not believe that anything would come between them, but he felt uneasy.

Mother Lewis, in her flannel nightgown, met him at the top of the second-floor landing.

"Oh, you're home early, son. Did you have an enjoyable evening?"

"I guess, Mother. . .but this civilian life takes a little getting used to." It was all he could think of saying as he went into his room to ponder the future.

* * * * * *

Saturday, December 24, 1864. . ."Kate left this morning for New York where she hopes to get a school. Went with her as far as Albany. Feel lonely and blue."

Charles had written a letter to the War Department office requesting procedural details on re-enlistment, noting that he had previously been offered a commission as colonel of a colored regiment. He had enclosed a certificate endorsed by Dr. Pease, vouching for his complete recovery from the illness which had forced him to quit the service. Surprisingly, word came back in less than 10 days that he had only to fill out the enclosed application and his case would be reviewed "as quickly as we are able."

While he did not expect to be called for examination for at least a month, Charles told Kate what he had done.

"You are the first to know, sweetheart, because it is my solution to what has been bothering us. The army has been good to me, the pay is better and I know that I am a good soldier. This war can't last too much longer and when it is over, we can be married and live on a military base."

Kate was not overly receptive to this turn of events, and she told him so.

"If that is what you want, Charles, I shan't stop you. I had thought there would be no more sleepless nights, worrying about you in the field, possibly dead or wounded. We've both lost loved ones and you have been injured and taken sick in this war. . .yet you choose to go back. It was my wish that you would remain a civilian and we'd be married before the war ends, but I can see that is not for us."

A week later, Kate reciprocated with the shocking news that she, too, was leaving Schenectady. She had decided to quit her job at the Niskayuna school and had already accepted a teaching position at a four-room school in New City, Rockland County, just north of the Bronx suburb of New York. Charles was devastated and hardly knew what to say, but Kate made it easier by reminding him that "good or bad, we've made up our minds to be separated from each other and our dilemma. . .and now it remains to be seen whether our love is strong enough to bring us back together."

It was a sad time for Charles, the morning of the day before Christmas, when he accompanied Kate by train to Albany. As he left the coach, to wait for the return trip to Schenectady, Charles could not hold back the tears and neither could she as they kissed and squeezed hands. He watched her train depart and grimly walked down to the waiting room.

Now that Kate had gone, and had said little more than "Goodbye, Charles, take good care of yourself" as they parted, he found himself doubting his own good senses.

In his diary the next evening, there was this terse entry: "Christmas Day; but not very merry."

Chapter 18
Advice to the Lovelorn

> *Thursday, February 23, 1865: "Received a letter from Col. Ed Ripley; he wishes me to come down to Washington, pass an examination for the position of Lieutenant Colonel in a Negro regiment, and again enter the army. I should like to, above all things, and will if the matter can be arranged."*

Since Kate left, Charles was leading a different sort of life. He and Bob Payne, also discharged from the army as a war casualty, had struck up a warm friendship and were out several nights a week. Sometimes they were down at Drullard's Hotel bar or at Herb Blesser's saloon on lower State Street, quaffing beer and trading stories with the clientel.

Charles also saw no harm in asking Phoebe Potter, a friend of the family, to accompany him at a program at St. George's. Several nights later they went to Anthony Hall to hear a concert by the renowned pianist Louis Gottschalk. Phoebe's brother Nelson came home on leave the following week and the three of them went out to dinner.

His mind was set now on rejoining the army. He had two letters from Colonel Ripley of the War Department, one suggesting he come down to Washington for a written examination, the other informing him that it wasn't necessary. He would be commissioned a lieutenant colonel in a colored regiment and was expected to report to the department in Washington on April 1.

At least that much in his life was settled — but he couldn't get Kate out of his mind. He had told the family about his plans after Kate left. Strange, he thought at the time, but none of them were unduly astonished. Father Lewis, in particular, told him "It may be for the best. . .you must get over this restlessness, son, before you can settle down."

On the night of March 13, Charles joined a party going by train over to Albany to see John Wilkes Booth, starring at the Gaety Theatre in his favorite vehicle, "Hamlet". With him were Phoebe and Nelson Potter, Bob Payne and two acquaintances visiting from Rochester, Jennie Franchot and Annie Cole.

On the return trip, the train was delayed for some time near West Albany and Charles found himself engrossed in conversation with Annie, who was a good listener and, he thought, extremely perceptive. She was a good-looking young woman, in her late twenties, with an engaging smile and eyes that twinkled as she spoke. After they had talked awhile, seated together in the train coach, Annie sat back, suddenly serious, and nodded her head as if she had made a discovery.

"Forgive me, Charles, if I may seem presumptuous in saying this, since we hardly know each other. . .but I seem to detect a certain sadness in the way you speak, even the look in your eyes. That should not be for a man who has returned safely from a hell on earth. Don't misunderstand. . .you have been delightful company and I should be proud to be with you again. . .but is there something that is bothering you?"

"I really didn't think it showed, wearing my heart on my sleeve, but you're remarkable in detecting it, nonetheless," said Charles, surprised by her frankness but impressed with the sensitive way she put it. "Yes, Annie, I do have — or did have — a girl to whom I was engaged up until Christmas. Her name is Kate. I still love her deeply, and I'm sure she feels the same about me, but she is gone and soon I expect to go back into service. That's about it. Now we live in different worlds, each of us going our own way."

Annie studied him for a moment, her lips pursed as she made up her mind.

"I'm going to ask you something, Charles, and you can tell me it is none of my business if you wish, but would you mind telling me what it was that could possibly separate two people who still love each other?"

"No, I don't mind really, and I thank you for whatever interest you may have in the lives of two virtual strangers . . . but it will be a boring story, I warn you."

"Try me."

The train was still motionless and the others were towards the back of the coach, laughing and talking, while Charles poured out the details of his broken engagement. He didn't want it to sound melodramatic, but when he had finished there was momentary silence — as between final curtain and applause. Annie sat quietly, looking out the car window, before she turned to Charles and stared at him intently.

"Listen to me, Charles . . . you may think me an awful meddler for what I am about to tell you, but I'm going to offer you some advice. Whether you heed it or not is your own affair. I've known you only a few hours this day, but somehow you have become a friend I shall always cherish . . . and that is why I hope you will at least consider what I have to say.

"Charles, first of all, you must begin to stand firmly on your own two feet. You have been listening to your family and their concerns about you, failing to recognize that in trying to placate them, you have been alienating your betrothed. You are a man, Charles, a soldier who has cheated death numerous times. . .not a boy who must listen and obey all that his father and mother tell him. In this case, I think you are doing both them and Kate an injustice."

Annie paused, placed her hand on his arm, then went on.

"But here is the advice. Knowing what you have told me, as a woman I feel certain that poor Kate is down there in New City this very moment, crying her eyes out and just praying that tomorrow's mail will bring a letter from you . . .asking forgiveness and that you wish to marry her as soon as possible. Charles, a love like yours comes by only once in a lifetime. If you shun it now, you will regret it to your dying day. Your main concern should not be your vocation. . .a man of your talents will be successful, I'm sure. . .rather it should be in claiming your soulmate and keeping her forever happy. Now that's all, end of speech and advice."

Just then, the car jolted slightly as the engine started up. Bob, Phoebe and the rest came to join them and they were back at Schenectady station by 10 p.m. The others went their way down Union Street while Charles headed up toward campus. He had already thanked Annie for her concern and invited her to dinner at the Givens the next night before she returned on the late train to Rochester.

* * * * * *

Charles was bright and cheerful at dinner, and Annie remarked he had lost "that look of doom".

"And why not? I took your advice and last night, before bed, I wrote a letter to Kate. It wasn't long, but I told her I had suddenly come to my senses and wanted us to get married before I go down to Washington. I'm still going back to the army but we will be husband and wife whatever happens after the war. I hope you are right, Annie, and she will be writing back a big 'Yes'!"

"Oh, I'll be right, Charles. I'd be terribly surprised if I'm not. . .but I hope that you told her it was entirely your idea?"

"Yes, of course, and if this works out as I hope it does, someday I will tell Kate about Annie Cole, the girl to whom we owe much gratitude. You are a young lady, yet you have wisdom far beyond your years, Annie. You've opened my eyes from a blindness of my own stupidity, and I don't know how I can ever repay you."

"Bosh, Charles. . .and now I must confide a secret of my own. Seven years ago next month — and I remember it to the day — I was foolish enough to listen to my aunt and uncle, with whom I was staying since a young girl. I was deeply, truly in love with a young man who wanted to marry me. The only thing was, he didn't want to stay in this state but wanted to homestead out in Iowa. My aunt and uncle were dead set against it, said it was risky and senseless to go out in that 'God-forsaken country'. He begged me not to listen, but to go with him and have a life together in new territory. I didn't go with him, Charles. . .and now you can see that I am not so wise after all."

Charles kissed her as she boarded the 9:20 westbound.

"Annie, my dear friend, I will write you soon as I have news. . .and I only ask that you let me know when your world brightens as well, as I'm sure it will."

Charles Lewis as Union College sophomore in early 1862

Capt. Charles Lewis in 1863

Rev. Peter J. Quick of New City

Barbara "Babbitt" Peissner in 1864

Chapter 19
Wedding in New City

March 29, 1865... "New City, Rockland County, Kate and I were married this evening by the Rev. Peter J. Quick, Mr. and Mrs. Blauvelt witnessing. The reverend gentleman expressed some surprise at the son of Dr. Lewis coming way down here to be married, but notwithstanding his wonderment, made no objection to performing the ceremony, and not to taking the $20 fee I paid him.

"And now I am a married man, with the duties and responsibilities attached to that position. I wonder if the change is fully realized by me. Heaven grant me ever a truthful loyal spirit toward my bride; make me ever faithful in word and deed. Kate has shown great trust in me, and deserves a good husband. God help me to be such to her."

It was an anxious week for Charles, awaiting the reply from Kate in answer to his plea that she forgive him for "my utter stupidity in harboring any doubt that we should be married soon. . .my darling, you have only to write and say you still wish me to be your husband, and we shall be wed before I report to the Washington office on April 1."

Would she take him back or had she already made up her mind to follow another path? He hadn't heard from her in nearly two weeks, and that was a short letter telling about her school work and the little town of New City, signed "Most obediently". This had to be, he told himself, the "crossroads of my life."

The weather was warming in Schenectady. Some heavy rains early in the week preceded a thaw which lifted the ice in the Mohawk River. The flood waters rushed by in grand style, carrying Volney Freeman's old bridge from its abutments. Farther upstream, big crowds gathered about the Schenectady and Scotia shores to watch the great jumbles of ice floes batter the covered bridge between the Washington Avenues that had withstood similar onslaughts since 1809. The heavily timbered span shuddered, shook and creaked from time to time, but it stood firm once more as the ice jams thinned out by March 18.

The next day, six days after he had taken Annie Cole's advice, there was a letter in the Lewis's postal box on the South College entry which was addressed to "Maj. Charles F. Lewis" — and was, unquestionably, Kate's handwriting. There were two other pieces of mail for him, but Charles pocketed them as he started up to his room clutching the one important missive he was almost afraid to open and read.

He had only to see the opening lines to know that he should never have doubted Katie's love and forgiveness: "My loved one. . .I thought my world had ended until yesterday, when your letter was slipped under my door here at the Blauvelt's and I eagerly opened it, hoping you would just say you missed me and wanted to come down to see me. But, oh, my dearest, how my heart took flight when I read your words, full of love and longing, just as I should have written many weeks ago."

Yes, she wanted to be married "as soon as you say you can be down here", and there was brief mention of his decision not to tell his parents until after they were wed.

"If you think it best, Charles. Under the circumstances, it seems our wedding will be quite a private affair. . just for the two of us."

Kate said she was sorry he could not stay long after the ceremony, but understood more fully his reluctance not to leave the service until the war had ended. Her letter, nearly three pages full, teemed with love and excitement which Charles felt as he read her words several times over. Already she had planned where the wedding might take place, at the parsonage of the local Reformed Church she had been attending. And they would stay at the Blauvelt's and her room for the brief while they had together, "until such time when we might desire a honeymoon trip."

* * * * * *

Charles kissed Kate tenderly as the Blauvelts smiled benignly upon them. The simple ceremony had been performed in the drawing room of the parsonage. Rev. Peter J. Quick, a tall, thin man in his sixties, was suffering from a head cold and he sniffed and coughed his way through the marriage rites, occasionally pausing to wipe his eyes. He stood beside lacy fronds of house fern which thrived in a wicker stand by the bay window. His wife stood to one side.

Kate wore a fawn silk gown with brocaded ruffles at the bodice and along the hem of the hoop skirt. Her honey-colored hair, parted in the middle, hung in soft ringlets on either side. She carried a small bouquet of violets, something Charles picked up at the Peekskill station.

"A bride never looked more radiant than you, my darling," Charles whispered as he held her close during the carriage ride back to the Blauvelt's boarding house. She sat quietly in the fold of his arm, then turned her face up to his and kissed him.

"A bride never was happier than I," she said softly.

A heavy rain drenched New City all the next day. While his new wife went to teach school, Charles remained in the tiny room which Kate had rented from the Blauvelts since she arrived there Christmas eve.

He wondered how she put up with the meagre conveniences. A huge double bed almost filled the room, crowded by other such furnishings as a wash-stand, a badly marred chest of drawers and a marble-top stand on which Kate had stacked a number of textbooks. It also served as her writing desk.

One of the wooden blinds outside the window had come loose and rattled whenever a gust of wind struck it.

Charles tried sitting downstairs, but the Blauvelts soon drove him back up to Kate's sanctuary. The landlady's clacking tongue and her husband's catnap snores were too much for him.

About 10 o'clock Friday morning, less than two days since they were married, Charles and Kate shared a goodbye kiss but vowed they would soon be together again. It was part of their agreement. Knowing that he had to keep his appointment in Washington and she had to finish the semester at school, they promised not to let this parting spoil their happiness.

"We are husband and wife now," she said. "These past few hours, Charles, have been heavenly and just knowing I will be back in your arms to stay gives me comfort enough to wait till that time comes."

Charles untied a rowboat down at a small dock where he had left it Wednesday afternoon, and rowed back across the Hudson. He had rented it from a boathouse on the Peekskill shore after getting off the train. Now, he waited at the tiny station nearly two hours before the train puffed into the yards and ground to a halt beside the platform. Only Charles and another man boarded, so the conductor signaled a quick departure.

"It's been a long run since Buffalo about midnight," he sighed, as the two hopped aboard. "We had to put on more coaches several times, and most of them are filled with recruits. Could be the war is about over. . .everybody is rushing to join up and get the bounty."

While he didn't think much of their reason for enlisting, Charles was ready to forgive the latecomers if they were right about the war's ending, even if it could be within the year.

He stayed overnight in New York City and would leave by train early the next morning for his April 1 engagement at the war office. And that night he penned a letter to Mother Lewis, announcing his marriage to Kate. He knew that she and the others would be surprised, possibly hurt, at what would seem a rash decision. . .but at this point, all he cared about was how much he and Kate meant to each other.

A popular 1864 engraving of President Lincoln

Chapter 20
The War's End

April 3, 1865. . ."Today everyone was startled with the news that Richmond had fallen, and Jeff Davis and the Rebel army were in full retreat with Grant pressing closely on that rear. This in my opinion virtually closes the war, and now the question paramount with me is, what am I to do? I'll get into bed, I guess, and think it over."

Leaving his bride in New City, Charles Lewis had arrived in Washington the afternoon of April 1 with the intention of signing terms of his re-entering the army with a promotion to lieutenant colonel, then moving on to camp. But instead of proceeding directly to Petersburg as expected, he was told that no passes could be issued because of heavy fighting going on about Richmond. Therefore, he was compelled to remain in Washington at least for several days.

He registered at the Metropolitan Hotel for the first day.

Then he took up residence at Shaffer's rooming house at 493 11th Street after a chance meeting with Sam Koontz, a former classmate at Union. Charles was sauntering down the avenue on his second day in the capital city, deep in thought about Kate and the army situation, when he brushed shoulders with a passerby.

"Charley Lewis! Wha — what the hell are you doing down here. . .hob-nobbing with the office brigade? I heard tell you made it big in the army, soldier, so where's the uniform?" the heavy-set man exclaimed, fervidly shaking hands and grinning ear-to-ear.

"Whoa, whoa, there Koontz. . .slow down a bit and give me a chance to recover from the shock! I haven't seen you in three years and there's a lot to tell. Right now I'm here on business, just what kind I don't know, but that's a long story. If you know of a good restaurant in the vicinity and are on the loose, what say we talk about it over dinner?"

Koontz, after listening intently to what Charles had to say about re-entering the service, shook his head as he waggled a forefinger at his companion.

"Charles, m'boy, you've patriotic spirit to spare and I admire you for it — but now's the time to start thinking of your own life, yours and Kate's both. The word around here is that the war's coming to its bitter end, praise be, and soon this city will be crawling with ex-officers looking for jobs they feel should be given to them just for the asking. My advice to you, Major Lewis, is to bend your efforts now to getting a good peacetime job before they're all taken!"

And Charles listened with renewed interest as Koontz told him there was a good chance he might get him an "in" with some high-ranking people in the

105

Treasury Department, where he had been working for nearly two years. He hadn't graduated at Union, either. He was rejected for army service on physical disability, so he decided to leave college and go down to Washington for "civvy work in a war capital."

Charles checked in at Olney Shaffer's rooming house, a room right next to Koontz, and that night wrote letters to Kate and Maggie. It had been quite a day, one that opened up all kinds of possibilities as to how he might spend the rest of his life.

* * * * * *

His mind was made up the next day after another visit to the war office and a brief talk with Colonel Ripley. From all indications, victory for the North was close at hand and the need for commissioning any more officers was slim to none. The colonel hadn't much time to spare. He had been working at the office most of the previous day, a Sunday, and had slept overnight on a couch.

"Things are moving so fast down there, we're hard put to keep up with general orders," he said. "Grant's getting everything he wants to wrap this up, and all of us up here are working practically around the clock. The President has been stopping by frequently, I think to make sure we aren't sleeping on the job."

Later that afternoon of April 3 came the news that Richmond, the Confederate capital and symbol of so much, had been taken and the Federal armies were rapidly in pursuit of the retreating, starving Army of Northern Virginia. These were exciting, delirious times for citizens of the North. People were running about, shouting and laughing, even gathering in churches that were open for prayer and thanksgiving. The war, nearly four years old, was not quite over but close to its last gasp. That night, the papers told of President Lincoln's decision to go down to Richmond, only hours after it had fallen, and walk the streets in celebration of the hard-fought victory.

Next day, Koontz came back from work ebullient with the news that he had talked with Judge Lewis, commissioner of U.S. Internal Revenue, about the possibility of an office position for Charles.

"Just by chance, I had to go up to his office today. I figured it'd be a good time to test the waters. All I had to do was mention your father's name and his face lit up like daybreak! He knows him and has often spoken of him, he said, and would like to see you. . .by God, Charles, maybe I'd best have you put a good word in for me!

It was a surprise to Charles that the judge knew his father, no relation. But on the other hand, he was becoming convinced that Professor Tayler Lewis was no slouch in the company he kept through the years.

After submitting a formal application for a job at the Treasury Building, Charles went to an interview with Judge Lewis on Saturday morning, April 8. The latter spoke hopefully, Charles thought, even intimating that he should have an appointment in a few days. That night he wrote in his letter to Kate: "My fingers are still crossed, but it looks as though everything is working out even better than planned. What more glorious development could take place than to have the war end, my becoming a civil servant, and to have us begin our married life in a nation at peace?"

Lee's surrender at Appomattox was reported the next day. The war was not entirely over, but it would come in a week as General Johnston and 37,000 Confederate soldiers asked for terms from General Sherman, receiving the same as was given the Army of Northern Virginia.

April 13 was the day chosen for the "illumination" of the capital. That evening, the city was ablaze with light from gas fixtures that had been installed in nearly every public building and around the concourse. Every street lamp was turned to full capacity and private homes throughout the city were brightened with gas lights and oil lamps set in front windows.

That night, while marveling at the beauty of the illumination, Charles and Sam Koontz stood near the dark pile of the Treasury Building where Pennsylvania Avenue gave an unobstructed view of the city all the way up to the elevated site of the Capitol, its newly completed dome glowing like a jewel against the darkening sky. Koontz remarked that it was a symbol of victory.

"Considering all that we've been through," said Charles, "With God's grace, I look upon it as a symbol of peace."

Friday April 14.

It is near midnight, & I have just come in from seeing enacted a tragedy, which will ring down through the ages, "till time shall be no more": the assassination at Ford's Theatre of Abraham Lincoln, the President of the United States. Seward is reported fatally stabbed, and all sorts of fearful rumors are afloat, while the city is in a state of excitement bordering on madness. Lincoln was shot in his private box, by, it is supposed, the actor J. Wilkes Booth. He is now lying in a house just opposite the theatre, in an unconscious state, & the Drs say there is no chance for life. Koontz & I were at the theatre & sat in the Dress Circle only a few feet from the box: saw the assassin enter it, and saw him leap from the box on to the stage & dart behind the scenes, after the commission of the awful deed. Secy. Seward was in his bed, sick, at the time of the attack & his son Fred. is said to have been badly hurt in trying to defend his father. What an awful ending to all the

A tragic account of Abraham Lincoln's assassination from Charles Lewis' diary on Friday, April 14, 1865.

Chapter 21
Tragedy at Ford's Theater

Friday, April 14, 1865 . . . "It is near midnight, and I have just come in from seeing enacted a tragedy which will ring down through the ages 'Till time shall be no more' — the assassination at Ford's Theater of Abraham Lincoln, the President of the United States. Seward is reported fatally stabbed, and all sorts of fearful rumors are afloat, while the city is in a state of excitement bordering on madness. Lincoln was shot in his private box by, it is supposed, the actor J. Wilkes Booth. He is now lying in a house just opposite the theater in an unconscious state, and the Drs. say there is no chance for life . . ."

Charles and Sam Koontz left the boarding house shortly after six and walked over to 12th Street for dinner in a small restaurant, a ground floor entrance down to a dining room which faced out on the slate sidewalk. As they sat at a table near the front window, their only view was of the legs of those passing by outside.

"We've a good hour and a half before curtain time," said Koontz, hoisting a glass of ale. "Here's to a relaxing evening, but more . . . a toast to your new job at the bureau."

At the moment, Charles was more elated over the turn of national events than the prospect of a civilian job, but he joined Sam's enthusiasm.

"Yes, and here's to our president and our country, soon to be reunited."

It may have been the aftermath of yesterday's great celebration, signaling the end of a gut-rending civil war. In any case, there was no frivolity as the two men sat down to a meal of overly-done veal steaks, baked potatoes, black-eyed peas and parsnip. They talked about the state of affairs and the glowing promise of peace in a land that had been so badly split over political and social issues.

Charles, though still two months shy of 21, was the veteran soldier who had seen more than two years of combat and many men die. He began to talk on and on about battles, useless loss of life because of poor field command, the tenacity of Rebel soldiers, and Lincoln's much-criticized regard for showing leniency toward the South when it was all over.

So it was Koontz, the civilian public servant, who could appreciate fully the impact of this moment to his dinner partner. And it was Koontz who, long after finishing his meal and lighting up a cigar, finally leaned forward with both elbows on the table, his chin cupped in his hands.

"Well, Major, I don't mind your going on about the war and how we must now bind our wounds and even forgive the enemy," he said with a sly smile, "but for now I believe we should turn our attention to getting our asses over to Ford's if we intend to join old Abe and Ulysses this night."

Charles clapped a hand to his forehead, realizing he had been hogging the conversation with his unadulterated enthusiasm over the war's end. "I must have sounded like a preacher . . . I'm sorry Sam, I went on so."

"Oh what the hell, Charles, you've earned the right. There's been a lot of flag-waving going on these past few days, but the guys who were in the field deserve the honor of being in the front row."

It was well past seven-thirty, now less than a half hour before curtain time, so the two men headed over F to Tenth Street and Ford's Theater. Washington's streets were especially alive with roisterers this night, still in wild jubilation over the war's end but more than that, an inordinate feeling of relief which showed itself in brotherly love. Strangers took time to slap shoulders, shake hands and even hug each other as they passed by.

"This has gotta be a time to remember. Geez, I can't ever recall when I saw a clerk thumping his boss on the back and getting a smile in return," Koontz said, cocking a thumb at the two they had just passed. He knew them both from the bureau, one a stock clerk and the other a supervisor. "I swear, if Jeff Davis were to show up tonight, they might even kiss *him*."

Ford's Theater, a three-story brick structure, loomed before them, fronting on a narrow brick sidewalk and an unpaved Tenth Street. It had been the site of a church, the First Baptist Church of Washington, built in 1833 but abandoned years later. John T. Ford, a Baltimore theater owner, happened to see the vacant building on a Washington visit in 1861 and thought it had possibilities as a theater. That December, he leased the place from the church board of trustees for five years with an option to buy. Ironically, it was gutted by fire a year later. Now Ford got a bargain, or so he thought. He bought the property for a song and used the existing walls for rebuilding a new theater, one he named Ford's Atheneum.

Just across the street was a rather unimposing three-story dwelling, made of common brick with curved stairway and iron railings leading up to the front entrance. There was a "Room for Rent" sign in an upstairs window. The owner, William Petersen, a tailor, had little trouble renting out the rooms to actors or transient soldiers because of its central location. In a few hours, its lower right apartment would be crowded with dignitaries in a solemn death watch, one of the most celebrated in history.

* * * * * *

It was a pleasant, cool night for this Good Friday's outing. A light wind, blowing gently from the southwest with temperatures in the upper 50s, wavered the flames of black tar torches set in metal barrels at intervals along the streets. As Charles and Koontz came up to the theater entrance, they

learned for the first time that General and Mrs. Grant would not be in the presidential party.

"They just got word, direct from Grant hisself, that they had some other engagement. Oh well, that's his business . . . maybe he didn't like the play!" a bystander offered, chuckling over his little quip.

As they went in, they passed a big poster still advertising "The appearance tonight of our esteemed President, Abraham Lincoln, and heroic Union Army General, Ulysses S. Grant, as guests of the theatre." They passed through a central doorway and were directed by an usher to a small set of carpeted stairs to reach their seats in the second-story dress circle.

"I told you these were good seats," Koontz gloated, as they settled into plush chairs right center, not 20 feet from Box Seven to be occupied by the honored guests. The pit orchestra already was playing an overture, the house was nearly filled and gas lights along the sides glowed dimly. No one was in the State Box, decorated for the occasion with bunting of the national colors and a blue Treasury Guard flag, a framed picture of George Washington in the center.

As his eyes became adjusted to the semi-darkness, Charles spied a familiar figure walking down the right-hand orchestra aisle to a seat near the front. It was, unmistakably, that of Gen. Ambrose E. Burnside, who failed at trying to convince Lincoln he was the man to lead the Army of the Potomac to certain glory. The general was in full uniform, replete with sash and military ribbons, but Charles was not impressed. "There goes another of our famous generals whose ambitions were mightier than their deeds. He must be here to bask in Abe's sunshine."

"Our American Cousin" began promptly at eight as two young blacks in red satin breeches came out through a flap in the curtain, then lifted both sides of it as they walked slowly to each end of the stage. Miss Kay Hart and E.A. Emerson were on stage speaking their lines when Charles pulled out his gold watch, squinted his eyes in the semi-darkness to note that it was just after eight-thirty. Must be that the President, too, had decided not to attend, he thought.

Suddenly, however, there was a buzz of voices throughout the gallery and the actors on stage began applauding as the Lincoln party was making its way into the private box. Professor Withers hurriedly raised his baton and the orchestra began playing "Hail to the Chief". Dimly, the figure of President Lincoln could be seen at the right of the box, partially hidden by drapes. With him were his wife and a young couple, Maj. Henry R. Rathbone and his financee, Miss Clara Harris, daughter of Sen. Ira J. Harris.

The entire audience — all 1,675 paid attendees — stood as one, facing the box and cheering wildly, as the orchestra continued to play the presidential salute with a flourish. Finally, Lincoln stepped to the front of the box, bowed and waved a hand in acknowledgement of the greeting, then gestured with both hands for the people to be seated and the show continued. With some difficulty, the actors managed to pick up their lines and the theater settled down to enjoy the rest of the production.

There was a brief interlude, when the house lights went up after Act One, and Charles glanced over toward the presidential box. He could see three persons plainly but the fourth, "Father Abraham", was but a dark figure seated in the shadows farther back to the right. It was a short intermission, and soon the gas jets were lowered and the play was resumed.

It was just after 10 o'clock, as the second scene of the third act had begun, when Sam Koontz nudged Charles. He nodded in the direction of a man moving gracefully down the right-hand aisle of the dress circle and up the broad steps leading to the boxes. "Some big shot, too busy to get here on time," Koontz whispered. "Well, better late than never, they say."

* * * * * *

A great roar went up from the audience as actor Harry Hawk, as Asa Trenchard in the play, looked after a departing Mrs. Mountchessington and declared: "Don't know the manners of good society eh? . . . Wal, I guess I know enough to turn you inside out, you sockdologizing old mantrap!" He was then the only person on stage.

Intermingled with the laughter was a popping noise, as though someone had just burst a paper bag, but few heard it. However, in a matter of seconds there was a disturbance to the right, at the State Box, which diverted everyone's attention. A slightly built man, brandishing a dagger, was leaping from the box railing, after a brief grapple with Major Rathbone. In so doing, he caught the spur of his right boot in the bunting and fell sprawling onto the stage, about eleven feet below. He arose quickly, and ran, limping on the outside of his left foot, to the wings and disappeared.

All were dumbfounded. Charles and Sam saw the man jump and fall, then run from sight across the stage, not knowing what had happened up in the president's box. Then they could perceive a bluish haze drifting from it into the auditorium and heard a piercing scream from that direction. "Water! Water!" someone cried. Major Rathbone, his left sleeve torn and bloody from a knife wound, suddenly leaned from the railing and shouted: "The president's been shot!"

Now they were lifting doctors up from the stage, since the corridor to the boxes was crowded with people curious to know what had happened and an attempt to get into Box Seven found the door jammed.

Near pandemonium reigned in the theater. The gas valve had been turned up, illuminating faces etched in horror, anger and disbelief. The aisles were packed with patrons who had now left their seats and wandered, some toward the stairs and the street, others toward the stage and the State Box. Many, both men and women, were sobbing openly. Everyone seemed to be asking the same questions — "Who did it?" "Was he stabbed?" "Was he shot?" "Will he live?" "Did anyone see what happened?"

At that point, no one seemed to know, except that word was getting around that the assassin was none other than John Wilkes Booth, well known to the theater people and outsiders as well. Koontz, for one, told Charles right after the man jumped from the box and ran from the stage: "I know who that was . . . it was John Booth the actor! Why that goddammed son-of-a-bitch!"

Theater ushers and security guards began pushing onlookers toward the stairs. "Please, please," they shouted, "The show is over and you can do no good here! Please make room for those helping the president!"

It took maybe a half hour before the theater was emptied of patrons who, only minutes before, were guffawing at funny lines in "Our American Cousin". Out on the street, there was a huge crowd gathering around the theater. Word had spread quickly about the shooting and now outsiders were mingling with the theater-goers, sharing whatever news they may have heard or made up. Adding to the trauma of the attack on Lincoln was news that other would-be assassins had set upon Secretary of State Seward in his home and that he, and perhaps his son also, were stabbed to death.

The night seemed endless to Charles, and he kept hoping it was a nightmare from which he would awaken shortly and mop his brow in great relief. Inside the theater, a staff of doctors still attended the president. Some who were the last to be ushered out said they heard that he was still alive but there was not much hope for his recovery. There was a hush as military men lined up outside Ford's entrance to make way for a party which carried the prostrate president, not on a stretcher but with hands locked beneath him, across the street to the Petersen house. Hats were removed and people blessed themselves at the sight of President Lincoln's bared head and long, swinging legs as he was borne tenderly by grim-faced men.

The stricken leader was carried to a back bedroom of a small first-floor apartment that had been occupied by William T. Clark, a discharged army private. The room was about 10 by 15 feet, soon to be crowded with doctors, family and officialdom. It was decorated with a brownish wallpaper, embellished with white figures, and furnished with a regular sized single bed, a bureau with wash stand, a rocker and ladder-back wooden chair. So it was here that the death watch began and where, in a few hours, a voice cried out, "Now he belongs to the ages!"

'Til after seven the next morning, the crowd would remain in the street between Ford's Theater and the Petersen house, waiting for the sad news they knew must come. How the public mood had changed in the span of a few hours! Earlier that night, they were happy the war was over and ready to accept Lincoln's policy of forgiveness for the South, good will toward all men. Now it was death to the assassins, get tough with southern sympathizers everywhere, and make the South pay for this atrocity. They also accused the Ford Theater management of implication, to the point where hotheads were shouting, "Burn it down . . . burn down the theater!"

It would take some time before the situation was understood, before the reasoning of Abe Lincoln's conciliatory attitude toward the South was fully appreciated.

Charles and friend Sam decided to leave the scene near midnight and went directly to their apartment. They said little on the way, shaking their heads in consternation. At the conclusion of his diary entry for that day, Charles wrote:

"What an awful ending to all the talk and hopes of reunion, peace and good will between the two sections of our unhappy country."

Chapter 22
A City Bereaved

Saturday, April 15, 1865... "The telegraph has just flashed news of the awful tragedy last night to the remotest corners of our land. Our country yesterday was a scene of universal rejoicing over the return of peace, but today it is immersed in gloom and clothed in mourning. The President died at 7:20 this morning, never having regained consciousness. Secretary Seward it is thought may recover, though his injuries are severe and are of course doubly serious from his weak condition. I cannot but feel that that the death of Lincoln is an immeasurable loss to the country at this time, and to no portion will his death be more serious than to the South. It will almost certainly change the temper of the North from kindliness if not invictiveness.

"Many a day will pass before we will again see in the White House the peer of Lincoln. In every sense he was a noble man, and in his life and conduct well exemplified the remarkable words of his inaugural, 'With malice toward none, and with charity for all; doing the right as God gives us to see the right.' I am young and perhaps incapable of correctly judging their excellence, but to me at least there is nothing in all of English literature that surpasses in beauty and in striking force Lincoln's speech last summer at Gettysburg and his late inaugural address . . . "

The change in the appearance of Washington City this morning was startling. The streets, with nearly every house and building already heavily draped in mourning crepe, formed long black avenues, and the hushed, awe-struck manner in which every conversation was carried on was in sharp contrast to the noisy hilarity of the few days before.

Charles had spent a fitful night, finally getting some sleep before he awakened at near ten. Before breakfast, he went to a newsstand down the street and got a copy of the two-page extra of the New York Herald, printed at 8:10 a.m. Its column rules were heavily edged in black and featured a large engraving of President Lincoln on the front. Underneath was a copy of Secretary of War Edwin Stanton's dispatch: "Abraham Lincoln died this morning at twenty-two minutes past 7 o'clock."

It told of the attack on Lincoln the night before by the "alleged assassin, Wilkes Booth" and of that perpetrated on Seward and son Frederick at his home. In his rush from the theater, Booth, who was brandishing a dagger at the time, dropped his hat and the lethal weapon — a small brass pistol. It was identified as a derringer, a 44 caliber, six-inch, single shot weapon which fired a heavy lead slug about the size of a marble. This was the bullet which entered

Lincoln's head from behind the left ear, lodging in the brain, doctors said. The news account also told of a search that had been made at Booth's lodging, turning up evidence that the murder had been planned as early as March 4. Actress Laura Keene, it said, had "definitely recognized the assailant as John Wilkes Booth, a rabid secessionist".

Charles, after reading the paper, did little of consequence the rest of that day. Koontz suggested they go down to Reilly's saloon and drown their sorrows. "We can't bring back the dead but maybe we can help ourselves forget why they had to leave."

Instead, Charles decided to go for a long walk and be by himself. He strolled for hours, went at a leisurely pace along the grand concourse and stood for awhile as he admired the great capitol dome far in the background, gleaming in the mid-day sun. It was on the steps of this building where Lincoln gave two inspiring inaugural addresses, the first when the dome was unfinished but soon completed, despite the war, at the president's urging.

As he ambled back toward Madison Place and the White House, Charles thought of Secretary Seward and his family. Surely, the news would have reached Schenectady by now and his father probably was distraught, not only of the attack on Lincoln but on his old friend William Seward as well. It would do no harm, he told himself, to at least inquire at the residence even though that household probably was in a turmoil.

This he knew for sure as he approached the Seward house, a big stone building nearly across from the White House that had been known previously as the Old Clubhouse. Soldiers were stationed in front of the dwelling and next to the doorway as well. Charles approached one of the men, a corporal, who immediately stepped forward, musket in hand, with an order to halt. It was apparent that, under the circumstances, the city now was under martial law.

"My name is Major Charles Lewis, and I am concerned about the welfare of the Secretary and his son Frederick, the Assistant Secretary," Charles explained. "I am well aware that the situation calls for tight security, but is there any way I can get some information on their condition? It is very important to me because the Secretary is a good friend of my father."

The corporal conferred briefly with his partner, then one of them went up the porch steps and into the house. In a few minutes, he came back out and, holding both palms outward, informed Charles that absolutely no visitors were allowed.

"I'm sorry sir, but these are orders. However, I can tell you that both Secretary Seward and his son Frederick are alive though frightfully injured, mostly by knife wounds . . . but the doctors say they both have a good chance of recovery. Sorry sir, but that's all I can tell you."

Charles was grateful for this bit of information and he felt relieved that perhaps part of the dastardly plan had failed. Later he would know that it was young Lewis Paine, a slow-thinking giant, who had burst into the Seward home and wounded not only the Secretary and his son, but three others in the

The funeral procession of Abraham Lincoln on April 19, 1865 as it moved slowly up Pennsylvania Avenue from the White House to the Capitol building.

house as well. Only one, Bud Hansell, a State Department messenger, would die as a direct result of the wounds.

He came back to sit on a bench at Lafayette Square where he had seen Lincoln only a few days before. The White House, just beyond, was draped heavily in black and inside, Charles presumed, was the new president, Andrew Johnson, who had been sworn in this day.

It was not only the death of Lincoln and the turmoil it had caused which occupied his thoughts.

"Kate, dear Kate . . . I miss you so and I need you now. If only you were in my arms, even if for a little while, my mind would be at ease once more," he mused with a deep sigh.

It was a lonely, confused young man who walked ever so slowly back to his lodging that late afternoon. Why should life, even death, be so complicated?

* * * * * *

April 18, 1865 . . . "Today with Koontz viewed the remains of the President, lying in state at the White House. He looks perfectly natural, and his manly, homely face is the picture of repose. Oh! 'The deep damnation of his taking off'!"

It was Palm Sunday on April 16. In Washington, as in most cities of the North, the churches had larger attendance than they would on Easter the following week. Hearts were heavy, in need of spiritual uplifting, and places of worship became the fulcrum for this support.

Charles walked over to the Unitarian Society and heard a powerful sermon by Dr. Channing on the assassination, emphasizing the irony of Lincoln's death on the threshold of peace and reunification of the nation. It was up to the living, he said, to bring the dead President's desire for absolute forgiveness and humane treatment of the South to fruition. Worshippers, both men and women, wept unashamedly throughout the service.

Two days later, Charles and Koontz joined the long lines waiting to enter the White House for the viewing of the martyred leader. The next day, they saw the long procession of the funeral cortege and military units up to the Capitol, where the ornate coffin rested on a canopied bier underneath the great dome. The following day it would be started on its long journey back to Springfield, Ill.

Time seemed almost suspended that whole week, as activity was held to a minimum, bereft of liveliness. Charles received notice to appear before the examining board of the Treasury, however, and he did so with some trepidation the day before Easter. When it was over, he was uncertain about his chances of landing a job.

"There were a lot of sour faces staring at me as I answered questions about some things I was vague about," he told Koontz that night. "Their expressions didn't change, either, even as I was leaving. I was told that the verdict should be in about Monday."

It was Koontz, actually, who came back to the apartment on his lunch time Monday to give Charles the good news. Judge Lewis, he said, had already heard that the board was impressed with the applicant's qualifications and had approved his appointment. A messenger stopped by that afternoon with notification of the approval and asked that he report to the Internal Revenue Department's main office in the morning.

So, on April 25, Charles began employment as a clerk engaged in official correspondence, at an annual salary of $1,200. It was a coincidence that the chief clerk in the office was a brother of the student Johnson who had a foot smashed by the cars in Schenectady.*

He was pleased with the work and his ability to grasp it quickly. Whether it was the environment or the subject, Charles found it more challenging than his previous experience in a law office.

* * * * * *

The joyful letters which came back from Kate, following news of the start of his citizen career in Washington, gave Charles further confidence that he had, at last, found his niche in the business world. They counteracted letters each from father Lewis and sister Maggie who were disparaged over the unannounced marriage. Mother Lewis sent a copy of the wedding item which appeared in the Daily Union, along with a brief note wishing them both happiness.

His father's words, in particular, bothered Charles and he sent off a letter in reply which afterward he thought might have been too severe. He wrote that night in his diary: "I hardly deserved such a letter I think, but I am sorry I answered it as I did tonight. Still, it is gone and I am too proud to take it back."

Annie Cole's advice the month before still was not forgotten.

In his letters to Kate, Charles kept asking if she could find some time from her school routine to come down to Washington "even if for a few days". After he had told her about the Grand Review celebration being planned for Monday, May 22 — an event which was to feature all Union armies marching together for the last time as a final tribute to the war's ending — Kate surprised him.

Not only would she be with him for the occasion, but "for all time, evermore." The New City school had just over a month to semester's closing and she had arranged for a substitute teacher for the final two weeks. She had given her notice of resignation and planned to join Charles on May 19.

"My darling," she wrote, "I feel strangely ethereal, as though I am floating in space with angels singing all about me. I shall indeed be in heaven when you are with me."

The next week, Charles was able to find a furnished apartment on Missouri

*See "The Johnsons of Union College" page 139.

Avenue, corner of 4 1/2 Street, which he was sure would meet with Kate's approval. The rent was high, $12 a month, but for its size and location, the place surpassed any he had looked at. There was a good-sized front porch to sit upon, shielded by vine-covered trellises. Inside were a large sitting room, dining room, spacious kitchen, two bedrooms, a bathroom, and a back porch which looked out upon a well-kept yard. The furnishings were old but clean and of good quality. He was sure Kate would want to make some changes in the curtains and draperies, which looked faded and seedy, and he would not interfere with anything she wanted.

The landlady, Mrs. Humphrey, lived in the apartment upstairs. She seemed a friendly sort, even to allowing the newly marrieds to "move right in, just as soon as you've a mind to . . . it's all neat and clean, waiting for you." Charles decided to move the following week, a few days before Kate's scheduled arrival, so he gave notice to Shaffer and began taking his meagre belongings to the new quarters. Koontz said goodbye "as a fellow lodger, but I hope not as your best friend at the bureau."

Kate arrived at the Washington train station Friday night, May 19, and rushed into Charles' waiting arms with an unladylike squeal. She had only a small suitcase and a grip with her, explaining excitedly that the Blauvelts promised to send her books and other belongings to "wherever Mr. and Mrs. Lewis might decide to set up housekeeping here in Washington."

"That's mighty nice of them," Charles smiled, still keeping the apartment a secret. "Come, let's get some dinner, my sweet. You must be famished and I just want to sit and look at you." Off they went, out of the depot, he carrying the baggage with one arm and embracing her with the other.

It was after 9 o'clock when they left the restaurant, some five blocks from Missouri Avenue, and Charles suggested they go for a stroll.

"It's a warm night, Katie, and before we go back to my room I'd like to show you the beauty of Washington just after dark." It was that, and the two young lovers walked slowly uptown, stopping occasionally to enjoy the view from a park bench. They they came to Missouri Avenue, where Charles said they might want to look for prospective housing in the residential section.

Kate was impressed with the sizable, clean-looking houses and their big front porches, but thought they "must be terribly expensive, at least for us just now." At the corner of 4 1/2 Street, Charles could contain himself no longer. He pointed directly across the street to the brick and wood two-family dwelling, the glow of the curbside gas lamp reflecting from the glass in the big front doors.

"Tell you what Kate, my arm's getting a bit tired lugging these bags and I think we've done enough meandering about town this first night. I've got a key here in my pocket which I am sure fits that downstairs door . . . what say we try it?"

Washington City was kind that night to its newest resident family. Both Kate and Charles vowed it was the most splendorous, romantic place in the universe.

Chapter 23
An Ending, a Beginning

> *May 24, 1865... "This day may be like no other in my entire life It swept before me three years of unforgettable memories — of tragic or glorious times in the field, uncertainties as to my own esteem and worth to those I love, the loss of dear friends and the acquisition of new ones, and ... not least of all ... the knowledge that through it all, I will have earned the right to be called a man when I become 21 in three weeks' time. Seeing my comrades of the western armies march before us today has reminded me that a lifetime can be crammed into a few short years. I pray to the Almighty it shall not be in vain."*

It was a hectic, bustling week in the nation's capital beginning Sunday, May 21. Hotels and boarding houses were filled to capacity and citizens everywhere with a spare room had rental signs in their windows. It was the week of the Grand Review, drawing friends and relatives of parading soldiers from all states of the victorious North.

Government work was slowed because of preparations for the week's activities and Charles was surprised, then amused, when Chief Clerk Johnson put him in charge of "adornments of the facade" of the Treasury Building. It consisted of organizing a search party for flags, bunting and signage to decorate the front of the big stone structure. Nothing extraordinary, Charles soon discovered. The city was accustomed to celebrations and the manpower, decorations and ladders were readily accessible.

However, he did encounter some difficulty in arranging display of a Confederate flag over the Treasury Building's front entrance. He insisted it would be appropriate, inasmuch as this was an occasion honoring those who marched, fought and died in a civil war — the vanquished as well as the victors. At first there was opposition, but after consultation among the top brass, the idea was accepted with the proviso that the stars-and-bars be positioned much lower than the national colors.

This was not the major problem which confronted Charles at the beginning of that week. He had written about the upcoming Grand Review to both sister Maggie and father Lewis a week before. He told them that the 119th Regiment would be marching with the 20th Corps on May 24 for the final parade and that he and Kate would be on the sidelines "cheering for Peissner's boys for all our worth."

He was dumbfounded Monday morning to receive a letter from Maggie saying that she and the children would be coming down by train to Washington to help pay homage to Elias and his comrades. Charles was visibly upset when he showed Kate the letter.

"Whatever made her think we can find accommodations at this late date?

We have our tickets for the reviewing stands, too late to look for more, and every available room in the city is filled with visitors! She and the children are arriving in the morning . . . what can I do, Kate?"

Kate smiled gently and put a hand on Charles' arm.

"Now, now, my dear . . . I'm sure it will be all right. We don't have to sit in the stands, there is all of Pennsylvania Avenue. As for accommodations, we have room aplenty for them right here. Charles, think a moment. This will be a day that Maggie and the children will always remember and cherish for the rest of their lives. Would you, could we, ever forgive ourselves for denying them that privilege?"

Charles said nothing, but reached over and enfolded Kate's face within his hands as he kissed her. He could not find the words to express the love he felt for her.

"I'll be at the station tomorrow morning at ten-fifteen . . . and we'll all have ourselves a bang-up time!" he finally said, smiling in admiration of his bride's sagacity.

Charles was granted permission to go down to the railroad depot in time to greet the Schenectady visitors as they came off the platforms. Maggie had at last shed her widow's weeds, now dressed in a mottled blue-and-white gown with a wide-brimmed hat to match. She was glowing with excitment and gave her brother a lengthy hug, despite the fact that they were blocking traffic in a busy corridor.

Little Tayler stood shyly in back of sister Babbitt, the two of them in awe of the big station and their mother's outburst of affection. Finally, Charles was free to take them to one side and welcome them to the big city while waiting for the baggage wagon. Tayler, who would soon be four, quickly warmed up to his uncle's smiles and comments. His eyes grew wide and glistened when Charles asked them what they wanted most to see while in Washington.

"We come to see Daddy's big parade!" he shouted with arms upraised.

Kate came running out when they arrived at the house in a depot horse cab and saw to it that the children were properly welcomed.

"You are all very special to us, because you're the very first guests in our new house!" she told them, then began strolling up the front walk with Maggie, arm-in-arm. Charles sensed he was no longer needed, so excused himself and went back to work.

* * * * * *

This was the first of two days of military parading. Today was entirely given over to the Army of the Potomac, while tomorrow's marchers would be the western troops famed for the March to the Sea. There was little to be done at the Treasury office and a skeleton crew had already completed the day's work, therefore Charles was excused from work until Thursday.

Kate and Maggie preferrred "some tea and women's talk" to seeing this day's parade, so Charles walked with the children over to the upper section of

Pennsylvania Avenue where the eastern soldiers were scheduled to come by within the hour. Luckily, they were standing outside a meat market when Charles struck up a conversation with the owner. The sidewalks were jammed with spectators, anxiously awaiting sight of the first division, and the man commented that the children would have difficulty seeing the parade. Charles agreed, but said he would "take turns with them on my shoulders."

"Nonsense," the other replied. "I closed my shop because no one will come in during the parade. But for you and the kiddies, I make an exception." With this, he unlocked the side door and they walked up to the second floor front. The children sat on the wooden awning overlooking the street and the men watched from the windows.

It was a great show, lasting for hours. The spit-and-polish Army of the Potomac did itself proud with freshly-laundered and pressed uniforms, shiny boots, flags galore, and regiment upon regiment marching in precise cadence to the music of countless bands. Behind each division rolled the ambulances, wagon trains and caissons, the equipment spotlessly clean and horses groomed to perfection. The great crowds lining both sides of the avenue cheered lustily as each new division passed by.

"I only hope our boys will do half as well tomorrow," Charles thought to himself as they picked their way through the masses after the parade. "Maybe we didn't dress as well and it might not look as pretty, but by hell we didn't lack for fighting ability."

He needn't have been concerned. The "bummers" of Sherman's mighty army had bivouacked for several days at Alexandria on the other side of the Potomac. Some said it was because the western soldiers had become such hardened, undisciplined men in their celebrated march through Georgia and South Carolina that they might "take the town apart" if quartered for several days inside Washington.

This Charles knew was citizen talk. He had seen Harvey Collum, now a captain, and Arnold Hall, recently breveted colonel, Monday morning while getting the grand stand tickets at the war office. They were in fine spirits and said the men were anxious to "show what marching really is before they fold their tents and head on home." Casualties past Atlanta were quite heavy, enough to deplete the regiment of most everyone Charles might yet remember.

"But we're still the 119th, Charles old man," Hall said with a certain grimness. "Even when we all get back to peacetime jobs, there will be an attachment to the corps. Just you give us a hallo from the stands and we'll give you a special eyes right!"

* * * * * *

Charles gave the two bleacher tickets to Koontz, and on that Wednesday morning of May 24, he and the others walked over to Pennsylvania Avenue before eight. They were in the front row of crowds which lined the sidewalks the full length of the avenue, and were situated quite near the reviewing stand not far from the White House, when the parade got off precisely at nine. President Johnson and General Grant were seated in the center of several dozen dignitaries set to watch this vaunted Army of the West pass in review.

Down from behind the gleaming Capitol came Sherman's men, Uncle Billy himself leading the parade astride his black horse. Major General O.O. Howard was just behind him, as the two officers kept their mounts to a slow but spirited walk down the cobbled thoroughfare. The 15th Corps came first, interspersed with musical outfits of every description.

As they approached the reviewing stand, Sherman rode directly to the side and passed right by Charles and his party. The red-haired general's eyes were shining with excitement and pride, his mouth taut as though to hide a grin. By now, his steed was decorated with garlands strewn by onlookers. Then he dismounted and walked up to the stand to join Johnson and Grant.

Then came the men of the 20th Corps, their shoulders squared and bayoneted rifles in perfect alignment as they swung into long strides befitting an army that had literally walked its way though the heart of the Confederacy. They weren't spic-and-span as the marchers of the previous day, but the crowds looking on seemed to recognize that here was a fighting machine which cared not as much for looks as performance. The men wore loose blouses, black slouch hats with wide brims, and their boots were dusty, scuffed and worn. Their faces were lean, tan and grim as they kept disciplined eyes straight ahead.

Charles felt the excitement of thunderous ovations each time a new regiment passed by. With it too came strange sensations of loneliness, pride, sadness, and devotion. Kate must have sensed it. She drew closer to him, held his hand and squeezed it tightly without turning her head.

Now came the Second Division and Charles leaned down to little Tayler to warn him: "Look sharply now, lad ... your Daddy's flag will be coming by!" Maggie stood to one side, her arm clutching Babbitt in mutual tension.

A great ovation greeted the 119th N.Y. Regiment as it marched smartly down the avenue, fast approaching the spot near the reviewing stand. The color bearer strode several paces ahead of the others, holding high the tattered regimental flag that was stirred slightly by a gentle breeze. The yellow had faded and the white star in the center was dirtied from battle and marching dust. The legends sewn on the flag told it all: Chancellorsville, Lookout Mountain, Missionary Ridge, Dalton, Kenesaw Mountain, Resaca, Ringgold, Peach Tree Creek, Atlanta, Bentonville.

At that moment, the crowds suddenly grew silent, then thundered its applause as Colonel Hall strode before the regiment, his sword over the right shoulder. And it was then that Tayler stepped forward and stood at attention while he saluted the men passing by. Charles was moved by the boy's unexpected action, and he joined his nephew in tribute to Elias, Lloyd and others of the 119th who died under its banner. Maggie and Kate, their eyes teared with emotion, clung to each other while the regiment marched by.

Never, as long as they lived, would any of them forget that day.

Part of the 20th Corps parading down Pennsylvania Avenue, May 24, 1865, during the Grand Review.

Epilogue

The foregoing covered three crucial years in the life of Charles F. Lewis, recalled by several of his acquaintances as a "dashing young fellow with a mind of his own". His was not a scraping, clawing battle with life to make his mark. The second child and older of two sons of the eminent Professor Tayler Lewis of Union College, Charles had the advantage of an outstanding family and cultural surroundings as he faced on his own an experience fraught with danger and turmoil.

Charles' boyhood life is a bit sketchy. We know he was born June 14, 1844 in New York City, first attending a private school there, then completing his elementary and secondary schooling in Schenectady when his father accepted a faculty position at Union. Naturally, Charles entered the Schenectady-based college when of age, and that was in September of 1860. Thus he was only 16 years old when he began the "straight classical course" in a duly accredited college! Only the favored sons of well-to-do families could have such a start in life in those days when higher education was obtainable largely by those who did not have to go to work by age 13.

The diary of Charles Lewis actually begins in August of 1863 as he is about to return to the front lines after a summer's leave at home to recuperate from a wound suffered at Chancellorsville. Whether or not he had written earlier diary notes is unknown. Luckily, however, he was given to reminiscing in the diary which does exist.

He wrote often in his diaried accounts as to how he was "the greatest mystery" to himself, wondered about religion, often predicted his own death (as was allowable under the circumstances) and, most regularly, thought of "sweet, loving Kate and those sweet lips". The lad was in love, make no mistake, but between the lines ran a wonderment of whether he was deserving of her love. Whether out of self-degradation from a youthful "I'm not good enough for her" attitude, or as a result of certain indiscretions while in the service which he did not mention, it cannot be determined.

In the diary of Charles Lewis, a page has been torn out just prior to the entry for their wedding day. We can only surmise that the contents of that page were too personal and, when read later, either Charles or some member of his family decided to make certain that those details were never read by outsiders. At any rate, there seems to have been no hint of an impending marriage, and the suddenness of the entry, "Today Kate and I were married," comes too much as an afterthought.

Katherine Rosa Smith, the attractive and demure schoolmistress, was the daughter of Otis and Sarah Merselis Smith. She was born in Jefferson County on January 31, 1844, a descendant of one of the oldest Dutch famlies of that area. She was brought to Schenectady when a child and it was here that she received her education. In later years, she was to recall occasions when brightly garbed Indian chiefs came to visit her grandmother Merselis, remembering favors which the old lady bestowed upon them. When Kate was a small child, the language spoken at teas and social gatherings was a mixture of English and Dutch.

For all the haranguing over the sudden wedding of Charles and Kate, it took. And, from all reports, Charles made a good husband. He and his new bride remained in Washington, D.C. as he stayed at his job in the U.S. Treasury and Post Office departments. They lived there, in fact, for nearly 32 years. Their two children were born there — Edward Lewis on February 3, 1868, and Jane Keziah Lewis on December 31, 1874.

* * * * * *

The Lewises returned to Schenectady in 1896 and resided at 704 Union Street, one house from the east corner of Union and Lafayette Streets. When they came back to the old home town, there was no longer the huge family on the college hill. Instead, all but Margaret Peissner were buried in the college plot at Vale Cemetery.

Margaret Lewis Peissner, widow of Elias, died in 1904. Both of her children had been buried: Barbara (Mrs. Ira Nelson Hollis) in 1892, and Tayler Lewis Peissner in 1895. Professor Lewis had been the first to "pass the veil", a phrase often used by Charles in his diary, in 1877. And when he was gone, the Lewises moved off campus and took up residence just down the tree-lined hill at 722 Union Street.

The Lewises had always been communicants of St. George's Episcopal Church on Ferry Street. Now Charles, his wife Katherine and son Edward attended regularly, often joined by their daughter Jane Keziah and her husband, John A. Seede, a General Electric Company executive.

Charles Lewis' life ended on March 6, 1905 after a brief illness. The funeral notice in the Evening Star next day read: "Lewis, Charles F., at his home, 704 Union St. Funeral at St. George's on Thursday, Mar. 9 at 2:30 p.m."

Kate and Edward went to live with her daughter and son-in-law after Charles' death. Edward died June 11, 1908 at age 40.

Those who knew Kate in those later years said she was a typical "grande and proper lady" of the Victorian era. She wore a widow's hat over tightly drawn snow-white hair. As she was comely as a young schoolmarm, she was beautiful as an elderly woman. She kept up her social activities, mainly with the St. George's Auxiliary and as a board member of the former Old Ladies' Home, now Heritage Home for Women at 1519 Union Street. Kate died August 11, 1933, at her daughter's home at 30 Balltown Road. She was 89. The funeral service was held in St. George's Episcopal Church on Monday, August 14, and she was laid to rest that afternoon beside her husband's grave, and Edward's, in Vale Cemetery.

The last survivor of the Lewis family was Jane Keziah Lewis Seede. After her husband John died February 7, 1954, she moved down to 49 Washington Avenue to live alone in an apartment — not far from the spot where her maternal grandfather, Otis Smith, once had a broom factory at Cucumber Alley. She, like her mother, was very active in the St. George's Auxiliary and the Old Ladies' Home.

"Kizzie" Lewis Seede lived to be 80 years old. She died March 27, 1955. Her funeral was at 11 a.m. four days later in St. George's Episcopal Church. She was buried beside her husband in the Charles F. Lewis plot.

When she died, an administrator of the Seede estate was appointed to auction off the effects according to provisions in Mrs. Seede's will. She desired a major share of the proceeds to go to the Old Ladies' Home. In one of the trunks, this a battered barreltop relic, the auctioneer found numerous souvenirs, decorations and war memorabilia which obviously once belonged to her father. Among them was a dusty account book entitled, "My Civil War Diary".

Gravesites of the Lewises in the Union College plot of Vale Cemetery. From left are the graves of Edward Smith Lewis, Charles F. Lewis, Katherine R. Lewis, Jane K. and John A. Seede.

Appendices

APPENDIX I

The 11th Corps and the Battle of Chancellorsville

Address by Charles F. Lewis before the Burnside Post, No. 8, Department of the Potomac, G.A.R., Washington, D.C. on November 12, 1885:

"Commanders and comrades: In compliance with the Commander's request that I relate some incident of the war, the happening of which came under my personal observation, I have chosen an affair that has caused considerable discussion which, at the time of its occurrence and for a number of years afterwards, was, in my opinion, wholly misunderstood. Even now, the prevailing impression is one of error.

"I refer to the behavior of the 11th Corps at the Battle of Chancellorsville. The general impression was and still is that the corps in the engagement acted in a cowardly and disgraceful manner, and that the loss of the battle itself was due to the conduct of the troops composing it. That the defeat and rout of the 11th Corps on the afternoon of the 2nd of May, 1863, caused the loss of Chancellorsville, and made what promised to be a successful advance on Richmond a bad defeat of the Union Army, I frankly admit; but that the troops of the corps were in any wise to blame, or that they acted in any manner less bravely than any other troops would have acted under similar circumstances, I deny. Whatever fault there was, rested with certain of the commanders, and not with the troops.

"I was at the time a first lieutenant of the 119th New York Volunteers, a regiment attached to Krysannoski's Brigade, Schurz Division, and I will now briefly relate some of the facts that occurred on that unfortunate 2nd of May, to most of which I was personally knowing.

"The 11th Corps had the extreme right of the line and had, prior to the battle if my memory serves me right, occupied that position some thirty-six hours. We were strung along the Chancellorsville road in a single line. Not a breastwork was thrown up, nor the slightest preparation made to resist an attack, though ample time was had. We lay there doing nothing of moment than loafing, sleeping, cards, and story telling.

"During the early forenoon of the 2nd, General Hooker, accompanied by General Howard and their respective staffs, rode along the line and General Hooker, in my presence and hearing, said to General Howard, 'General your line is, as I fear, too greatly extended.' On the return of Hooker to his headquarters, he wrote and duplicated an order to Howard, and for this I have the word of Colonel Fessenden, a personal friend and a member of Hooker's staff, and who, unless I am mistaken, carried the order which in substance directed Howard to contract his line and be prepared for an attack from either front or flank.

"Not the slightest preparation was made, nor so far as I ever learned, was any attention paid to this order. Shortly before noon, a heavy dust became visible to us all, over in the direction of Fredericksburg and moving slowly towards our flank. It was remarked by both officers and men that this cloud of dust came from troops either retreating from Fredericksburg or moving for a position on our flank. If the former view was correct, why were we not moving to intercept; if the latter, why were not preparations made to receive a flank attack? Nothing was done, however.

"In the afternoon, about three or four, a captain of an Ohio battery attached to the corps, with two or three orderlies rode out beyond the right of the corps for the purpose, as I understood, of selecting some good site for his battery, the belief being that on the 3rd (of May) the 11th Corps was to move still further to the right, the 2nd Corps taking our place. The captain referred to, and whose name I think was Wheeler, rode beyond the extreme right but a comparatively short distance when running into a skirmish line. He lost one of his orderlies, wounded and barely escaped himself. On his return he reported the facts to Howard and stated as his belief that a large force was behind the skirmish line.

"His story was pooh-poohed and, under orders from Howard, the men were told to make themselves as comfortable as possible for the night. All danger of an attack seemed to be over; at all events, such was the impression created among the troops.

"Within an hour, or between five and six I think and while the guns were stacked and the men engaged in cooking and eating their evening meal, the attack, sudden and awful, of Stonewall Jackson's forces struck us. The guns of the 3rd Division, the division having the extreme right, were captured in their stacks. Neither a cavalry picket nor an infantry picket — nothing more, in fact, than a camp guard, was on the right flank of the great Army of the Potomac on that bloody afternoon to give warning of the approach of the swift-moving and great commander Jackson.

"The attack came just as the dust cloud had indicated it would come, on the flank and rear. The 3rd Division was rolled up and tumbled upon ours, the 2nd, in dire confusion. Our brigade had just time enough to get into line, face to the rear and make a left half wheel, when Jackson's men were upon us; and a grand though terrible and awe-inspiring sight it was that met our view.

"This was my first battle, but in all my after experience never did I see a more thrilling sight than the advance of that line of battle.

"On they came, four deep, as though marching by the flank, they had fronted without undoubling files, leaving open the spaces and pouring the shot into us by volleys. The front rank would fire and then apparently pass through the spaces, and thus become the rear rank, while the whole force slowly but steadily advanced. The line was a long one and lapped us on both ends, and why we were not to a man made prisoners has been to me always a mystery. Had we been older in the service we would have gotten out of such a death trap as rapidly as possible, but all of us were green — that is of this brigade — and we did not realize the hopelessness of our position or know enough to run. Besides, the frantic personal appeals of General Howard to hold the enemy in check until he could reform the corps on a new line held the men of the brigade up to their work until human courage and endurance were exhausted.

"Finally we fell back, leaving a line of dead and wounded heavier by far than the line that slowly and sullenly retreated, and thus ended our part in the Battle of Chancellorsville.

"I would not accuse General Howard of willful negligence or carelessness. It may all have been a mistake of judgment, and certainly no one could truthfully accuse him of personal cowardice or of a lack of patriotism — but that he woefully misjudged, and to that misjudgment and that alone was due the disaster and defeat of Chancellorsville, was my opinion then and is still.

"Hooker's disposition of the troops was excellent, at least we all thought so, and I have never seen any successful criticism on the general disposition made by him. I am not here, however, to defend Joe Hooker. He needs no defense. Every man who ever fought under his command knows the true, tried mettle of his makeup. But I have desired and attempted to do what little was in my power towards removing the unjust aspersions hitherto cast upon the troops of the 11th Corps.

"Never was a word of criticism directed against those troops before that day, although most of them were veterans in service. And certainly the record of the 20th Corps, half of which was composed of troops from the 11th, is as fair and bright as that of any other of the corps composing the army of General Sherman in his march to Atlanta and the sea."

APPENDIX II
Memorial Tribute from GAR

On January of 1906, a small package arrived at the home of Kate Lewis. In it she found a small book, bound with black leather embossed in gold trim. On its front cover, also in gold, was printed "Charles Frederick Lewis".

It was a tribute to Major Lewis, long a member of the Burnside GAR Post 8 of Washington, D.C., compiled several months after his death. The memorial, actually a glowing sketch of the officer's life, was written by A.F. Sperry of the Burnside post. Though parts of it may be repetitive of what has already been written, the tribute overall does reflect the esteem in which Charles Lewis was held by his comrades in arms.

"Charles Frederick Lewis was born in New York City, June 14, 1844; at the age of eighteen years entered the Union Army as Second Lieutenant in Co. A, 119th New York Volunteer Infantry on August 5, 1862; was promoted to First Lieutenant in December of the same year, to Captain on July 24, 1863, and to Major on May 15, 1864, and in August of that year was honorably discharged at Chattanooga, Tenn. by reason of sickness and wounds.

"Comrade Lewis took part in the battles of Wauhatchie, Missionary Ridge, Dalton, Rocky Face Ridge, Resaca, Culp's Tavern, Peach Tree Creek, Kenesaw Mountain and the battles about Atlanta, and in the Battle of Chancellorsville he was shot in the left arm, crippling him for life. Comrade Lewis joined the Burnside Post on May 8, 1882 as a charter member, and the foregoing facts are from his record in the post.

"The following are from data kindly furnished by his intimate friend, Judge H.A. Kelly of the Post Office Department and by Rev. Dr. Andrew V.V. Raymond, chancellor of Union University, Schenectady, N.Y., and from an appreciative article by Prof. Sidney G. Ashmore in the Union University Quarterly for February, 1905.

"Comrade Lewis was the son of Dr. Tayler Lewis, a distinguished theologian of the Dutch Reformed Church, who for many years and up to the time of his death was professor of Ancient Languages in Union College at Schenectady, in which institution Comrade Lewis was educated. Dr. Tayler Lewis himself was graduated from Union College in the class of 1820, among his classmates being Hon. William H. Seward, Judge William Kent and Dr. L.F. Hickok, afterward president of Union College. Dr. Lewis was the author of 'The Six Days of Creation', 'Plato Against the Atheists', and 'Commentary on the Book of Job'. At the time of his death, he was considered the foremost Oriental scholar in America.

"At the outbreak of the Civil War, Colonel Peissner, then professor of Modern Languages at Union College, recruited a company, of which eighty members were students at the college, and drilled them on the college campus until they left for the front. Colonel Peissner, brother-in-law of Comrade Lewis, was killed in the Battle of Chancellorsville.

"After being wounded and discharged from the army as major in 1864, Comrade Lewis came to Washington early in the following year with the intention of re-entering the army, but while he was waiting here, the war ended. At about this time, he married Katherine R. Smith, who had been a school acquaintance and who, with their two children, Edward and Jane Keziah, now lives at Schenectady.

"Comrade Lewis was in Ford's Theatre when President Lincoln was assassinated, and in an address before the Loyal Legion in this city, some five years ago, he made a valuable contribution to the story of that crime. In April of 1865, Comrade Lewis was appointed to a position in the U.S. Treasury Department in connection with the Bureau of Internal Revenue, where he remained until 1873, when his services were sought by the American Banking Co. of New York, in charge of the issue of internal revenue stamps. He remained with that company until 1877, and then returned to the Treasury Department as superintendent of the stamp vault of the Internal Revenue Bureau at a salary of $2,000 a year, which position he held until his father's old friend, Donald M. Dickinson, becoming Postmaster General, offered him the Chief Clerkship of the Stamp Division of the U.S. Post Office Department. This Comrade Lewis accepted on Feb. 15, 1888, and retained with honor until March 15, 1890, when he was removed for political reasons, the official who brought about this removal being afterward forced to resign.

"Upon leaving the Post Office Department, Comrade Lewis engaged in private business in Washington until Nov. 1, 1893, when he was made Post Office Inspector and assigned to the Philadelphia and New York Divisions. Later, at his own request, he was given the territory of Essex, Franklin, Fulton, Montgomery, St. Lawrence, Saratoga, Schenectady, Warren and Washington counties of New York, and he was engaged in his official duties until the disease, which gradually grew upon him, caused his death at Schenectady on March 6, 1905.

"Comrade Lewis's unfailing consideration for others was well exemplified in the following incident. He had studied law in the Columbian University in Washington and for many years had hoped for an appointment in the Department of Justice. A son of Postmaster General Howe, who had been his classmate at the university, came to him with an offer of the long-desired position, but the appointment meant that a certain veteran in the department must be displaced. The incumbent was an old man, presumably near the end of his usefulness; but rather than be the occasion of loss and embarrassment to another, Comrade Lewis declined the position.

"For the weak and even for the wrong-doer, Comrade Lewis's heart was full of sympathy. He was a communicant in the Episcopal Church, and the atmosphere of his home showed his nature and tastes as those of an educated Christian gentleman. His official services as an Inspector were so valued by the

Post Office Department that he was retained on its rolls to the last — a mark of confidence and consideration which he appreciated. When his last commission came, he thought he was better, but the light of gratitude in his face was in that of a dying man.

> *"Then who shall tell how deep, how bright,*
> *The abyss of glory opened round?*
> *How thought and feeling flowed by light,*
> *Through ranks of being without bound?"*

Kate's Reply

Within the memorial book that had been preserved through the years was found this copy of a letter which Kate Lewis sent to A.F. Sperry on January 19, 1906 in appreciation:

"Words are inadequate to express the gratification I feel for the memorial address to my husband, so beautifully made into book form by your own hands and sent to me. It represents delicate labor, a great deal of time, and much regard for Mr. Lewis. Could he but know of the attention, how pleased he would be, for the esteem of his fellow men, particularly of his soldier friends, was ever dear to him.

"Tell his comrades at the post they can add to his record that he was a soldier to the bitter end, and please say to them that his family individually thank them and you for the address presented at their 'Post of Sorrow'. Hoping I may sometime meet you and other members of the Burnside Post 8, I remain sincerely and gratefully."

Katherine R. Lewis

APPENDIX III
Civil War Potpourri

THE "SHEBANG" — This is a term coined during the Civil War which became a popular phrase in later years, one meaning posh buildings such as an elegant house. However, it began as a reference to establishments of the U.S. Sanitary Commission, built in various parts of the states — at first in the North but later in some of the southern territories taken over by the Union armies. The Shebang was something akin to the USO centers in World War II, where service personnel could find a place to write letters, partake of snacks, and even be given general information or advice on a variety of problems. During the Civil War, the Sanitary Commission provided aid and comfort to the Union troops, particularly the sick and wounded. Funds for the Commission were raised through "Sanitary Fairs" in the bigger Union cities and through individual contributions. The Commission thus was able to provide extra blankets, clothing, books, even boxes of candy for the troops in the field or aboard ships.

* * * * * *

"SEEING THE ELEPHANT" — Raw recruits in the Union armies were the first to hear this derisive phrase while they were in training or first on the line. What it really meant was that they hadn't seen the first battle, heard slugs whiz over their heads, never saw men fall dead or fired their own weapons at the enemy. The way veteran soldiers explained it was that you had to think back to the days when the circus came to town. Everybody back then, old and young, wanted to see the elephant, the main attraction. Once they had seen it, things changed for them. They had witnessed something they had never seen before, and they would never forget it the rest of their lives.

* * * * * *

LINCOLN VOTE IN SCHENECTADY — The Schenectady Daily Union and the Evening Star both came out with bulldog editions the early morning of November 9, 1864, newsboys roaming the streets about 4 a.m. shouting: "Extra, extra! Lincoln wins!" The news desks had finally gotten word that Lincoln was re-elected in his race with McClellan.

In Schenectady County, the president got 2,103 votes compared to 2,169 for "Little Mac". In Albany County, McClellan had a majority of 2,730. New York State's total vote was Lincoln 63,787 and McClellan 56,617. The electoral vote was 212 for the Republican President and 21 for Democrat McClellan, who carried only Delaware, Kentucky and New Jersey. The popular vote was 2,330,552 for Lincoln and 1,835,985 for McClellan.

* * * * * *

THE "COLORED TROOPS" — When the Civil War got into full swing and became extremely burdensome for both North and South by the end of 1862, black families truly found themselves in the middle of hostilities. They were "coloreds" in those days as they were often referred to up until recent years. The Emancipation Proclamation freed them from bondage, but most remained slaves in the South until the war's end unless they were able to escape. In the North, there was growing sentiment against the "coloreds" because they were viewed by hotheads as the cause for the war. Large scale reverses in the earlier campaigns added fuel to this fire as death totals were announced in the northern states. The five-day anti-draft riot in New York City in mid-July, 1863 involved the wanton killing and beating of many defenseless Negroes.

So-called "colored troops" began organizing in the North about the time of the emancipation and at first there was mixed reaction. One side, harboring strong racial prejudice, thought it "lunacy" to recruit Negroes in the Union Army, even if within their own units. A fast-growing popular sentiment, however, was that it was to the North's advantage to allow the recruitment of colored troops. The lives of more white men would be spared, more men could stay on their industrial jobs, and more quotas could be met if the Negroes were allowed to enlist. When the war ended, it was disclosed that about 180,000 blacks enlisted and served in the army and nearly 37,000 died as war casualties.

There was not, however, any disposition to have the "colored troops" self-sufficient to the extent that even their leaders would be black. The War Department made it clear they would have only white officers training and leading the black troops. Later in the war, a few black men eventually did become officers in colored troops.

When the black soldiers began fighting in the South, many wondered how the Confederates might react to their being in the battle lines. Only once, however, did the congressmen of the North investigate a possible "atrocity" against colored troops. Confederate Gen. Nathan B. Forrest's army attacked and captured Fort Pillow, Tenn., near Memphis, on April 12, 1864 and it was reported that most of the blacks in the federal stronghold had been massacred. Casualties were high, but records tended to show it was just war and not slaughter.

APPENDIX IV

The Johnsons of Union College

James Gibson Johnson was born in Providence, R.I. on June 25, 1839. He was a student at Union College, 1860-1864 (a member of Kappa Alpha fraternity), was at Princeton Theological Seminary, 1864-66, and ordained into the Presbyterian ministry December 27, 1866.

He served pastorates at Presbyterian church at Newburyport, Mass., 1866-1868; Congregational church at Rutland, Vt., 1869-1886; New London, Ct., 1884-1890; Chicago, Ill., 1891-1899; Farmington, Ct., 1899-1904. He died suddenly at Washington, D.C. on March 25, 1905. He was married to Mary Rankin of Newark, N.J., who died in Mexico a week before her husband. He was fatally stricken in a train near Washington while he was on his way home with her body.

They were married in 1870 and had four children: Eleanor, Rankin, Burges and Hilda. He was the son of Lorenzo D. and Mary Burges Johnson.

The above information was supplied by Prof. Burges Johnson, longtime member of Union College's faculty during the first part of this century. In a letter dated April 23, 1959 and written at his summer home in Stamford, Vt., he wrote the following in answer to our request for more information about his father:

"Let me put it as briefly as possible. My father was a Union graduate, I am not sure but I think he entered about 1860. He was the secretary of Mr. Seward, for, like many other young men of that day, he got a secretarial job in Washington. He was aided by his older brother who was secretary of another of Lincoln's cabinet. Seward, evidently took a liking to the young man and persuaded him to go to college and study law, and Seward would give him a job in his law office. So Dad went to Union.

"While at college in Schenectady, he fell under the influence of one of his teachers who persuaded him to study for the ministry. But while a student, he was struck by a railroad train and had part of one leg amputated. That kept him out of war, but he also got what he told me was then the largest award from the railroad which had ever been granted up to that time. That money paid for the rest of his college and also paid the college expenses of a younger brother who became quite a man.

"My father entered the ministry and I think that throughout a long ministerial life, few of his parishioners ever knew he had a wooden leg. He never told anything about that accident to us children, but I have often wondered if Seward hadn't a hand in those damages for Seward continued his friend for many years."

APPENDIX V

The Bounty System

In the beginning of the War Between the States, neither side really was prepared for war and for the first year and a half their main concern was building armies to fight full-scale battles. At first, both sides raised troops only by volunteers but it soon became evident that conscription must be resorted to in order to create standing armies. The South started first, in mid-1862, and the North followed in 1863 with a draft act that that could be invoked in any district where the number of volunteers lagged below a prescribed quota.

The practice of giving payments, or bounties, to recruits began at the outset of the war but it became an important tool of the enlistment centers when the draft law was enacted. Bounty payments appeared to favor the rich or those who wanted to avoid soldiering for any number of reasons. However, it was a plan whereby cities like Schenectady could raise money to be offered as bounty to those willing to sign up, thereby meeting the period's quota and eliminating the drafting of its citizens, rich or poor. It worked in Schenectady and in most other towns where bounty taxes were levied to meet the quotas.

This led to a sort of competition between counties, because those who were willing to sign up began to shop around for the highest bounty. It also created "bounty brokers", opportunists who went into the business of arranging for volunteers to get the highest amount offered in the state — with, of course, a small commission for themselves. There were also "bounty jumpers", the most despised of the bounty practice. These men signed up as substitutes, received their bounty payment and then would disappear either before or soon after they were assigned to a military unit. Often, they pulled this trick several times, but in different parts of the states. A few, but not many, were caught and sent to prison for long terms.

In Schenectady, recruits at first got a bounty of $100 for enlisting, but as enlistments slowed and Lincoln signed the National Conscription Act in April, 1863, the bounty rate was $300. The story of the draft and of substitutes or bounty brokers was the same in Schenectady as in most communities. The main thing was that the public was in favor of raising a suitable amount in taxable funds to keep the civilian wage earners, husbands or sweethearts from being caught up by the draft.

Probably the worst crisis in Schenectady in meeting the draft quota was in September 1864 when recruiting had suffered the "slows" and, despite a general public urging for a "show of patriotism", it appeared the quota would not be met. Many of the men scheduled to be drafted were family men. Several downtown businesses tried to cooperate by opening recruitment offices in their stores, but it was not enough.

What had hurt Old Dorp's enlistment quota was the fact that several neighboring counties had taken the initiative and increased bounty rates to upwards of $800 per man. Therefore, many eligible recruits from Schenectady County began to enlist elsewhere, where the going rate was higher. This was offset, in the nick of time, at a meeting in the Schenectady courthouse at 108 Union St. when County Treasurer S.V. Swits was authorized to borrow $175,000 through capital notes for the purpose of offering $975 to each recruit and $25 to each person who presented a recruit.

It had the desired effect. According to the Daily Star, "The streets were flooded with recruits at Capt. J.P. Butler's office at the postoffice, next to Drullard's Hotel. They were paid partly in cash, partly in county notes."

The specter of getting caught in the draft again hung over the city in April of 1865. The war was going well, the Union armies were over-running the tired, hungry and out-numbered Confederates, yet draft quotas still had to be met. The county funds were exhausted and now Treasurer Swits was offering county bonds to be purchased by private citizens for the purpose of building up a fresh bounty reservoir.

As late as April 4, 1865, several days at a time would pass without a single recruit signing for army duty. But on April 10, the day Schenectady was thrown into fits of wild celebration over the news of Lee's surrender, a news account read: "Everybody is anxious to enlist. Singular, isn't it? We are told Captain Butler had his hands full all day."

APPENDIX VI

Burning of the Church

In his "Schenectady County . . . Its history to the Close of the Nineteenth Century," (pub. 1902) lawyer and district attorney Austin A. Yates described the burning of the First Reformed Church building in 1861. He attained the rank of major in the volunteer forces of the Union Army during the Civil War. Following is part of his account of the fire:

"Just after the outbreak of the war, in the summer of 1861, a terrific fire broke out in Schenectady. At the site of the downtown storehouse of Yates & Mynderse at the foot of Cucumber Alley . . . was situated the broom manufactory of Otis Smith. A workman was repairing the tarred roof. In some careless way, the pitch became ignited on the northwest corner of the building and the fire ran down to a pile of dried broom corn brush. The flames rose at once in tremendous volume and it was about all the workman could do to get out of the way in time to save his life. A perfect gale was blowing, and the alarm was sounded by the usual yells and the ringing of the old Dutch bell, followed by those of other churches and the tooting of locomotive whistles, which was all the alarm then used. A tremendous conflagration immediately resulted . . .

"Urged by the violence of the northwest wind, the flames swallowed the dwelling house belonging to Otis Smith on the corner (of Washington Avenue and Cucumber Alley), cleaned up all that side of the street north to the bridge, and south swept away everything to, and including the house now occupied by Mrs. John Barhydt. So rapid and fierce were the flames under the gale that it was all people could do to escape with their lives. Great clots of fire swept through the air, alighting on roofs all over the town. Pretty soon there were more citizens on the top of their buildings than there were inside, for no house in the path of the wind from Washington Avenue east was safe.

"The five volunteer companies were hard at work (and) Albany and Troy were telegraphed for aid. They promptly responded and special trains brought engines. Steam fire engines were a recent invention. One (from Troy) was stationed on Front Street connected with one of the cisterns . . . The panic in the city was terrible. Washington Avenue from State to Union Streets became empty. Barns and houses out of the apparent path of the fire were freely opened to shelter the homeless and terror-stricken people.

"In the midst of all the excitement, there was a shout among the people who had packed every street in the west end of the city. There was a reef of fire around the clock in the old Dutch church. People were too busy preserving their homes and staying the progress of the flames to bother at that time with any church. It was a grand sight as the old building went to pieces, and was viewed with unconcealed joy by the pastor, who had been struggling and fighting for a new church for years. People (climbed) through the windows before the fire descended, and saved the cushions from the seats, or stole them, and, with a great crash, the bell, weighing nearly two tons, came down making more noise in death than it ever did in life. It was a blessing in the disguise of flame, for the present beautiful edifice quickly rose upon the spot."

* * * * * *

The Rev. Dr. Edward E. Seelye was pastor at the time of the 1861 fire, and it is written that he and the consistory worked diligently to plan for construction of the fifth edifice in that church's history. It was the first church in the Schenectady settlement, founded by the Dutch inhabitants in 1680. Dr. Seeley was among those participating in the dedication of the newly built church on August 6, 1863.

Kathryn Sharp Pontius, in her contributing section of the recent two-volume "The History of the First Reformed Church of Schenectady, 1680-1980", related an interesting sidelight to the placing of a weathervane on that new church building in 1863:

"In the 1860s, however, the First Reformed Church took several steps to counteract its public image as a Dutch church. When the architect of the fifth church building suggested in 1863 that the traditional chanticleer of the Netherlands churches be placed as a weathervane on the spire of the new edifice, Consistory voted, after due consideration, to go on record as 'wanting no bird nor fish on top of our church'."

Mrs. Pontius also recorded that by the 1880s, "the First Reformed church's desire to minimize its Dutch descent was reversed by the pageantry and nostalgia of its bicentennial celebration." It created within the church and the community a new pride in their mutual Dutch heritage. The Rev. W.E. Griffis highlighted this new feeling during his sermon at the 200th anniversary service in 1880.

Speaking of the beautiful new church, he mourned the absence of the Dutch chanticleer on the church spire: "The only fault I find in the details is that a meaningless arrow was put upon the spire, instead of that emblem which historically befits a Dutch church as it does none other, the cock of St. Nicholas, the symbol of life and resurrection, of the soul greeting the dawn light of heaven after the night and darkness of death."

When fire wrecked the Dutch church once more, this on a below-zero night of February 1, 1948, a new church was erected within the standing stone walls of the 1863 edifice. And when a new spire was erected a few years later, the traditional chanticleer became its weathervane.

The First Reformed Church of Schenectady as it looked shortly after its construction in 1864 to replace the one burned in the 1861 fire.